God wants to speak to you mor
Him. In *Listen Up! Hearing God at* ...... iviason
provide profound insights and practical advice, equipping you
to recognize and respond to God's guidance in your everyday
life, transforming your work into an act of worship.

John Bevere
Best-selling Author and Minister
Co-founder of Messenger International & MessengerX

Listen Up! Hearing God at Work by my friends Andy and Janine
Mason is a must-read, guide, and friend for anyone who desires
to encounter the words, works, and wisdom of Jesus in a new
way. This book is not an untried theory but a living experience of
how to hear the voice of God and obey it! Some books are read
and remembered, but a rare book becomes a life companion,
kept close at hand during the storms of life. If you are in ministry,
on mission, or in the marketplace (like me), consider reading this
book once a year for the REST of your life.

Dr. Leif Hetland
President of Global Mission Awareness
Author of twelve books, including *Called to Reign*
LeifHetland.com

Andy and Janine Mason are long-time friends and trusted leaders who have spent years equipping the body of Christ on the journey to know God and the depths of His Divine nature! In their newest book, *Listen Up! Hearing God at Work,* you will be activated through tools and exercises that help you cultivate your ability to recognize God's voice in your own life—and especially in your work. The truth is, He is always speaking. Can you hear Him?

Kris Vallotton
Senior Associate Leader, Bethel Church
Co-Founder of Bethel School of Supernatural Ministry
Author of fifteen books, including *The Supernatural Ways of Royalty*

Listen Up! Hearing God at Work is a brilliant compilation of biblical principles and powerful business practices that will prove that it is vital for everyone to hear God's voice throughout each day, and it is the key to success in your business or employment. As co-founders of Heaven in Business, the Masons understand what it means to live an intimate life-style with God and to walk in the fullness of Christ's authority without fear or compromising to cultural norms. I consider Andy and Janine dear friends, and I have witnessed them living, loving, and leading out of the power of the Holy Spirit because they can hear the voice of God. They are full of humor and insight and share powerful testimonies highlighting the impor-tance of drawing near and yielding to God. Come along on this new journey with them through *Listen Up!* and discover that not only is Jesus the way, the truth, and the life, but he also deeply cares about your business. He will lead you in wisdom and innovation to bring you into the abundant life he spoke about in John 10:10.

Reverend Joanne Moody
Agape Freedom Fighters
LIFE School, Agape Apostolic Equipping and Training Center

Andy and Janine Mason's *Listen Up! Hearing God at Work* is Biblical truth, vulnerable and transparent storytelling, and practical wisdom packaged together beautifully and powerfully for every believer who desires to experience God's best in business (and life). I will be recommending this book often!

Shae Bynes
Author, *Grace Over Grind*
Founder of Kingdom Driven Entrepreneur
ShaeBynes.com

Do you struggle to hear from God — especially at work? Do you ever wonder whether what you *thought* you heard was from God or just your wishful thinking? Do you want to know *how* to hear from God more clearly and act on what He is saying with more certainty? Then *Listen Up! Hearing God at Work* is the book you've been waiting for."

Ray Edwards
Author, Founder, and CEO
RayEdwards.com

Every believer in the marketplace seeks God's will before the planning begins, during the execution, and eventually in the evaluation of results. However, the fine line between hearing arbitrary suggestions and listening to specific directives remains blurred. In "Listen Up," Andy and Janine Mason take the reader on a voyage that begins with the foundation of active listening and ends with an application through informative steps of activation and influence. This book makes Scripture come alive as a workplace primer that reveals the intuition of God's voice and the implementation of God's will. The practical experiences through myriad examples of chronological success will keep you seeking and sensing the voice of God in your journey.

Krish Dhanam
Author and Speaker
KrishDhanam.com

For anyone seeking the edge in business, Andy and Janine Mason unveil the greatest secret for Kingdom enterprise—follow the voice of Jesus! God's voice releases the power to redefine reality and accelerate outcomes. Andy and Jasmine frame these helpful principles in a way that is accessible, biblical, and measurable.

Dan McCollam
Author and Trainer
Co-founder of The Prophetic Company &
Bethel School of the Prophets

In a world with more noise and distraction than ever before, Andy and Janine Mason have given us a key to hearing God in the everyday. This book will not only equip and energize you, but it will also position you to hear His voice at home, at work, and in all the places of your life. When chaos and confusion reign, we all need to hear clearly. Buy this book, study it well, and listen to the power of His voice to give you what you need to follow Him.

Dr. John Jackson
President of Jessup University
Author of *Grace Ambassador*

"Eternity is waiting, watching what you do next..." From the very first word in *Listen Up! Hearing God at Work*, I was riveted by how profoundly simple and true the words leaping off the page felt for me. Andy and Janine Mason take hearing God's voice from a concept available to an elite few to a reality that is accessible to everyone! It is easy to understand in practical terms while also opening your heart to desire an ongoing conversation with God.

Hajara Pitan
Head Coach, The Audacity to Soar
Lagos, Nigeria

Read Up! Andy and Janine Mason have crafted a wonderfully accessible and practical primer for hearing and responding to God's voice. This book reminds us that everyone can hear God, that hearing improves significantly with diligent listening, and that as we respond to what God is sharing, our Father releases life, carries peace, and makes His presence impossible to ignore. In a world overflowing with information but desperately short on encouragement and wisdom, this book reminds us to cut through the clutter by focusing on an audience of one.

Chuck Proudfit
President of At Work on Purpose
AtWorkonPurpose.com

Jesus said, 'My sheep know my voice...' Imagine a world where every follower of Jesus understood that they could talk with God, ask questions, and get answers about little things and big things. Andy and Janine Mason nail the simplicity of hearing from God in their latest book, *Listen Up! Hearing God at Work*. This book is a game changer for this country and worldwide, enabling Jesus-followers to walk and talk in fellowship with our Father just as Adam and Eve once did. So good! So relevant and so practical!

Jim & Martha Brangenberg
Talk Show Hosts
iWork4Him.com

Some books are read for head knowledge; some touch the heart; others are practical and implementable. Andy and Janine Mason's book *Listen Up! Hearing God at Work* takes what most would think is a difficult subject, hearing God's voice, and makes it simple, heart-touching, practical, and implementable in every aspect of life, including business. I highly recommend this book as well as attending a Heaven in Business workshop to fine-tune your listening ears to God and to be able to work alongside others who do the same. When I meet people who walk out what they teach, I want to keep them close. Andy and Janine are two of those people.

Ford Taylor
Founder Transformational Leadership
Author of *Relactional Leadership*
FordTaylorTalks.com

Andy and Janine Mason are powerful and important influencers in this hour. Their book *Listen Up! Hearing God at Work* will inspire and equip you to take your influence to the next level. This book is a resource that empowers you to ask yourself good questions, especially when trying to make the right decisions. It is filled with foundational truth, inspiring stories, and higher perspectives to help us see the bigger picture in all we're doing. I highly recommend this book.

Steve Backlund
Leadership Coach
Author of *The Culture of Empowerment*
IgnitingHope.com

The ability to know how God is speaking and what is being said is a fundamental way of learning and living out God's will. Andy and Janine have given you a treasure trove of golden nuggets to develop your ability and understanding of hearing God's voice. *Listen Up! Hearing God at Work* is filled with truths, a solid biblical foundation, and practical exercises that will enable you to apply what has been taught. All of this is infused with the inspirational testimonies of transformed lives. Biblical truths. Practical exercises. Inspirational testimonies. This is a perfect formula for transformational living!

Dr. Sharon Perry
Spiritual Director and Life Coach
Silent Retreat Facilitator

As a seasoned entrepreneur, learning to be led by the Spirit of God is a game-changer. Andy & Janine's book empowers you to discover and actively walk in 24/7 friendship with the Holy Spirit. This book will help you forge a deeper connection and partnership with all that Heaven has to offer you, and it's so much more than you can think or imagine. Get ready!

Matt Flegler
Founder Salt + Light Wealth Academy
Author of *How to Hear God at Work*
SaltLightWealth.com

Andy and Janine Mason have written something helpful to Christian business leaders and Christians alike. To take such a vitally incredible concept, like hearing God's voice and breaking it down in easy-to-read, practical steps, is incredibly helpful as the Church (community of believers around the world, not an organization) learns to step into the priesthood that God speaks about in the New Testament. This priesthood includes every believer, not just the ones with 'special' favor. A key aspect of being in that club is our ability to hear from God directly and trust what we're hearing to act on it. This book will help you move closer toward that goal.

Mike Thakur
Entrepreneur
Author of *Mike Drop*
MikeThakur.com

Deeply personal. Prophetically insightful. Profoundly doable. These six words succinctly describe what you experience as you read, study, and activate the wisdom within *Listen Up! Hearing God at Work.* I promise - you'll reread, review, and refer to this book for many years to come.

Dr. Jim Harris
Author of *Our Unfair Advantage*
Host of *The Unfair Advantage Show*
DrJimHarris.com

Andy and Janine bring clarity to the truths that every believer needs to be girded with as we steward our lives and talents while we walk this earth. May His voice ever become the loudest in your ears as you glean from *Listen up! Hearing God at work* and experiencing Him near and dear in your everyday.

Andrew Ng and Grace Chen
Serial Entrepreneurs
Singapore

In a self-expressive and overstimulated world that is aggressively seeking the unscathed truth, every one of us wants to get better at recognizing and listening to the voice of God. Each chapter of *Listen Up! Hearing God at Work* immerses the reader into a world where the Word of God and the voice of the Holy Spirit is central and exciting to daily life. This is not just a "business book"; it is a life book that illustrates powerful stories and gives practical tools for anyone with an "all-in-on-God's-plan" mentality. Whether you want more for your family, second guessing if you heard God correctly, or feel like you need to re-assess the people speaking into your life, this book is a game changer at turning the gray areas of unanswered questions into breeding grounds of anticipation.

Tommy and Rachel Deuschle
Entrepreneurs
Artisan Tribe
CMedia Africa
Stadium Worship

How much fun would it be to work with your best friend? The person who knows you best, knows your wildest dreams, and the one who could give you perfect wisdom and guidance. It wouldn't be like work at all. It would be like a dream come true! Learning to master this experience in your work life is what Listen Up! Hearing God at Work is about. I highly recommend this book as your next choice in building your business!

Danny Silk
Author of *Keep Your Love On*
and *The Way of The Dragon Slayer*
Founder of Loving On Purpose
President of Danny Silk Consulting

Listen Up! Hearing God at Work will help all believers, not just ordained ministers, to hear God in the midst of the busyness and conflicting priorities of everyday life. These practical insights on how to hear the voice of God will make hearing God's voice second nature to all believers and thereby turn their businesses into outposts of the Kingdom of God. "May your kingdom come" is more than a wish, and this book will help each believer craft an actionable plan to integrate that spiritual reality with the company's business plan. I highly recommend this book to all who seek to integrate their faith and their marketplace activities into one seamless whole.

Ken Fish
Former Fortune 500 executive
Author of *On the Road with the Holy Spirit*
Founder of OrbisMinistries.org

Listen Up!
Hearing God at Work

ANDY & JANINE MASON

HEAVEN IN BUSINESS SERIES

Listen Up!
Hearing God at Work

Cover and interior design by Hadassah Dowuona
HDowuonaDesignStudio.com

All scripture quotations, unless otherwise indicated, are taken from the New King James Version: copyright ©1982, Thomas Nelson Inc. All rights reserved.

ISBN- 978-1-7346984-1-1

To order more books or resources, email:
contact@HeavenInBusiness.com

Table of Contents

"I am passionately in love with God because He listens to me. He hears my prayers and answers them. As long as I live I'll keep praying to Him, for He stoops down to listen to my heart's cry."

PSALM 116:1-2 TPT

May you have eyes to see and ears to hear! Peace, Andy & Jaice Sept 2024

Foreword

In his book, "Jesus and the Powers," New Testament scholar NT Wright refers to Jesus' words in John 18, "My kingdom isn't the sort that grows in this world," replied Jesus. "If my kingdom were from this world, my supporters would have fought, to stop me being handed over to the Judaeans. So then, my kingdom is not the sort that comes from here." (John 18:36 NTFE) This translation captures something that many commentators gloss over. Yes, Jesus' Kingdom is not like the kingdoms of this world. It doesn't originate the same way or behave like the kingdoms of this world. But Jesus' Kingdom is still for this world, for the benefit and blessing of this world, for the redemption and rescue of this world.

Not many people I know carry the message of God's Kingdom breaking in now to bring about the redemption and rescue of the world, like Andy and Janine Mason. The pages of this book carry revelation, authority, and the fingerprints of the Kingdom of God for the sake of this world.

Unfortunately, the modern-day prophetic ministry has often become self-absorbed and fed a certain celebrity status that disables believers from the joy of stepping out in all that God has for them. This book breaks the super-spiritual status of celebrity prophets and helps *you* hear God powerfully and practically.

What is brilliant about this book is that it has been tried and tested. In a world where the church has often answered the wrong questions and looked for an escape plan, what Andy and Janine do is help demystify hearing God outside of the still, soft-playing ministry music in the sanctuary and bring God's voice right into the middle of your workplace, the time where you spend most of your working and waking life. As NT Wright says, "God's kingdom is not of this world, but it is for this world.[1] " God has solutions for your workplace and wants to reveal them to you. Andy and Janine help us hear Him more clearly.

The Masons are kingdom practitioners who have embraced the reality of partnering with God to bring his kingdom into all spheres of life. Their book Listen Up! Hearing God at Work is not only thoroughly biblical but also instructional and will unlock your senses and ability to hear God anywhere.

As someone who has been involved in active prophetic ministry for over 30 years now, taught about hearing God's voice countless times and worked with many business people, politicians, and creatives outside of the church context, I am always looking for healthy models of not only hearing God's voice and being quick to recognize it but also stepping out in what he is saying for the benefit of those around us.

Through their wise, practical activations and instruction, Andy and Janine help make hearing God's voice accessible and supernaturally natural. What's more, they do so with inspiring testimonies, helping us track how God moves so we are ready at any time for Him to do the impossible. Listen Up! Hearing God at Work is faith-filled without being religious or out of touch; it is honest and insightful.

Ultimately, what I love about this book is the call to step away with the Father, to get time with him, develop intimacy, and delight in all He is. The most significant cry I hear from high-level executives, Instagram influencers, politicians, and busy stay-at-home moms or dads is the overwhelming noise and anxiety that modern-day culture is producing. This book invites you into the communion of trinitarian intimacy and the joy of sharing it with friends and family around you.

This book is timely. It will help you silence the noise and rest in God's grace. He loves to speak to his children. Only abusive fathers intentionally stop communicating with their children. Hearing your father's voice is your birthright! And He wants to speak to you where you are: in your home, church, and workplace!

Read this book. It will do you good.

Julian Adams

Internationally recognized prophet, founding Pastor of The Table Boston, creator of Vox Dei: A Prophetic Lifestyle e-course, and author of Terra Nova: Your Call to Redeem the Earth and Make All Things New. JulianAdams.org

1. N.T. Wright. 2024. Jesus and the Powers: Christian Political Witness in an Age of Totalitarian Terror and Dysfunctional Democracies.

Introduction

We can't remember what each other's voice sounded like the first time we met. However, after 25 years of marriage, we can confidently recognize one another's voice across a dark, crowded, noisy room! We can tell if the other is happy, sad or angry. We often know what the other wants without saying anything – just one look is all that is needed!

It has taken years of listening to one another and responding or adjusting to develop a deeper confidence in knowing one another's voice. This has resulted in deeper friendship and intimacy, navigated disconnection and dysfunctional beliefs toward one another, and continues to grow... as we consistently and lovingly listen to each other's voices.

Similarly, we have grown in confidence in hearing God's voice. I (Andy) initially couldn't tell you if I was hearing God or last night's dinner! But as I leaned into daily reading His Words, I started to recognize His Voice. I started making decisions based on my hearing, and they proved correct! I learned the value of wise and godly counsel in working out the application and timing of what I heard. Then, there was a period in my late twenties when my confidence in hearing God's voice in a particular area of life was repeatedly challenged by contrary circumstances. At the same time, different leadership voices that I had deferred to in an unhealthy way knocked my confidence. But even through that period, I continued to grow in hearing God more than I realized. It forced me to go back to His Word and test if what I thought I heard was true.

Even better, that period when my confidence in hearing God was undermined gave me an unwavering resolve to strengthen others' confidence in hearing God. How do we ensure people are fully equipped to hear God's voice? How do we give them the keys and lessons that accelerate rather than hinder their journey to knowing what God is saying? How do we equip a generation to prioritize listening to their Creator's voice and navigating a world of good, bad, and impossible choices?

You are reading a book today because of the lessons we learned, the steps we took, and the perseverance we gained... over more than four decades. We have learned from outstanding spiritual leaders and mentors. We have also learned from poor leaders and poor choices! God has a way of taking all things and using them for good, and you benefit from it.

We have been praying for you. As you read the pages of this book, you will be accelerated in your experience of hearing and knowing your Creator God's voice. Even more so, our prayer is that you draw nearer and nearer to Him. That you would experience His immeasurable love and affection toward you. You would grow closer and closer to Him and walk in the fullness that He paid for you! "He who did not withhold His own Son, will He not freely give us all things?" (See Romans 8:32)

Eternity is waiting, watching what you do next. May you encounter more of His Voice on these pages and let history record you as a friend of God.

We can't wait to hear your story!

Andy and Janine Mason

How to Use This Book

Our greatest desire is that this book catalyzes you to do something. It's not simply a compilation of inspiring stories. We have taken the time to intentionally break it down into building blocks to help you practically grow in your connection with God and your confidence in hearing His voice. Here are a few practical keys to best use this resource:

1. Slow down and silence distractions.

In our fast-paced world, it's easy to get caught up in the rush of daily activities, constant notifications, and endless to-do lists. To fully benefit from this book, it's crucial to intentionally slow down. Find a quiet space where you won't be interrupted. Turn off your phone or put it on silent mode and allow yourself to be present in the moment. This will help you to focus and hear God's voice more clearly.

2. Grab a bible, journal, and pen.

This book is designed to be interactive. Having a Bible will allow you to reference and reflect on the Scriptures mentioned. A journal and pen are essential tools for jotting down insights, reflections, and any words you feel God is speaking to you. Writing things down can help cement them in your memory and provide a record to reflect on as you progress.

3. Read, then pause: do the activities in each chapter.

As you read through the chapters, you'll encounter various activities to help you apply what you learned. Take time with these sections, pause, reflect, and do the activities. This practical application is where real growth happens. Engage with the exercises and allow yourself the space to explore and experience God's guidance.

4. Continue to experiment, learn, and grow.

Hearing God's voice is a journey, not a destination. As you work through this book, be open to experimenting with different ways of listening and responding to God. Learn from your experiences, and don't be afraid to make mistakes. Growth comes from continuous practice and being willing to step out in faith. Keep trying, learning, and growing in your connection with God.

5. Do this with a friend.

A companion on this journey can provide encouragement, accountability, and a different perspective. Share this experience with a friend or a small group. Discuss what you're learning, your challenges, and the breakthroughs you're experiencing. This shared journey can deepen your understanding and support your growth in hearing God's voice.

Multiply This!

You are about to benefit from over forty years of our journey learning to hear and follow the voice of God.

People all around you are starving for someone to teach and train them in the same way.

So, here's what we are doing to help with this and how you can contribute.

We established the Hope Directive (charitable organization) to translate, multiply, and deliver training and resources to people with economically limited access.

We raise the funds to translate and reproduce resources like this book, then distribute these through trusted in-person relational networks and online platforms.

To join us in multiplying this training and subsequent ability for all to hear the voice of God, you can do the following:

1. Go to HopeDirective.com

or scan the QR code below and select "Multiply Resources" for your purpose-driven donation.

2. Email contact@hopedirective.com

with your request (and proposed distribution plan) to translate this resource into a specific language.

Placing tools in the hands of every believer, that results in Kingdom transformation.

Foundations
for Hearing God

CHAPTER ONE:

Three Truths to Hearing God

When God created Adam and Eve and gave them the responsibility to steward creation, He never intended for them to do it alone. The key to stewarding creation was connection with the Creator. Adam and Eve walked with their Creator in the cool of the day (see Genesis 3). Can you imagine what that was like? Take a moment to imagine what they talked about. What discussions would you have had if you had been face-to-face with the Creator?

Then, as the Bible tells us, Adam messed up by ignoring what his Creator, God, said and choosing instead to listen to lies. The result? Lost connection, lost authority, cursed work. Not cool, Adam!

Fast-forward to Jesus. The fact that God chose a redemption plan to humble Himself and come as a servant... as a human being, is beyond comprehension (see Philippians 2:7). Jesus grew up and had the power to do anything but chose to only live according to what He heard and saw the Father saying and doing (see Matthew 4:4, John 5:19, and John 8:28). Then He gave us the Holy Spirit, the Spirit of Truth so that we could live the same.

And so, we get to live happily ever after... sort of. We still have a choice to make every single moment. Will we live according to what we think alone or what we hear God saying?

If Jesus, the perfect Son of God, didn't live by what He thought by Himself but by the voice of God, how much more so should we? If He restored the original standard of living with the Presence and Voice of God in the cool of the day, what is the invitation to us? Could we have been living from a set of principles rather than a vibrant and ongoing conversation with our Creator?

Our greatest need is to learn to hear and know God's voice.

So, what is stopping us?

As we have worked with people over decades, we continually encounter beliefs and behaviors that limit God. In laying the foundations for knowing and growing by hearing God's voice, here are three critical truth statements we must understand and fully embrace.

1. Everyone can hear God.

"And other sheep I have which are not of this fold; them also I must bring, and they will hear My voice; and there will be one flock and one shepherd."
(John 10:16)

Kevin was the owner of an employment recruitment company and a devout atheist. The company had been with his family for 33 years but made a loss and incurred unsustainable debts for the last three years. In the process, Kevin's wife became a follower of Christ and began to pray for her atheist husband. In his own words, he "wasn't very cooperative, to say the least." However, at a particularly low point in the business, his wife challenged him to give God a try. Kevin agreed to listen to the "Voice" and do whatever it told him.

Kevin says, "During the initial weeks, the Voice told me who to fire, who to hire, and who to call for new business opportunities. As the weeks went by, I saw remarkable improvements in my business, and I could finally sleep. Still not accepting the realization that God was working in my life, I continued with life as usual."

"My wife's birthday was coming up, and I asked her what she wanted for her birthday. Her response was a total surprise; she wanted me to take her to Bethel Church (in Northern California) for the weekend. My initial response was, "NO WAY!" But the Voice said, "If you go, I will show you who I am, and you will be baptized." Since I had promised my wife I would listen to the Voice, and it had worked for me so far, I agreed to go."

During the morning church service, Kevin's wife turned to him, saying, "I'm going up the front to worship. Would you like to come?" Kevin said, "No." The Voice said, "You're going." Kevin obeyed and found himself at the front of Bethel Church with a crowd of expressive people raising their hands in worship. The Voice said, "Raise your hands." Kevin said, "No!" The Voice again said, "Raise your hands." Kevin again said, "No." A third time, the Voice said, "Raise your hands." This time, Kevin obeyed. As he lifted his hands, Kevin experienced the Presence of God, having a light-bulb moment connecting the Voice and God Himself. Later in the service, it was made known that there would be a baptismal service in the evening (Bethel only held baptism services once a month at that time). Kevin responded by becoming a personal follower of Jesus Christ and was promptly baptized.

Kevin's business is now more profitable than it was when he took it over from his parents four years ago. He continues to listen to the voice of God at work and throughout his life. His passion for the voice has also led him to help others learn to recognize the same voice. Kevin says, "I want to spend my life helping others take that same step of faith to give God a try. He will not let you down."

Kevin was a devout atheist, fully convinced that there was no God—yet he unknowingly heard the voice of God repeatedly. Even little children can recognize His voice. New believers and those who don't yet know Him can hear Him as well. Everyone has the ability to hear the voice of God. You, too, can hear God speaking to you!

When our children were young, we trained them to listen to God's voice. As a family, we would prepare for guests by asking God what He wanted to say to them. Our preschool and elementary-aged children would hear from God in simple yet profound ways and then draw pictures of what they heard.

Janine once had the opportunity to work with all the children in a Christian school as they asked Jesus what He wanted to show them about their school. It was beautiful to observe how the first graders received the same messages from Jesus as the eighth graders. They didn't have fancy language for what they were hearing or seeing, but they drew pictures of clouds of Glory surrounding the property as God spoke to them about what He wanted for the school.

When our son, Ben, was around nine, our family believed God to own a house in the United States for the first time. We kept having random people give us prophetic words about the house, and we felt like the season was getting close. However, nothing changed in our financial situation, and it still seemed very far away in the natural sense. One day, Ben came to us quite discouraged about the whole house situation. He asked us when we thought the house would become a reality. We had no answer for him. We didn't know what God was up to or when things would shift. Instead of giving him an answer, we encouraged him to ask God when the house would become a reality for us. Shortly afterward, Ben gave us a date that he believed he heard from God. And Ben heard right! The date he heard was when we found the house that would become our first in the United States. By then, we had the finances to buy it, and Ben also heard God say the price we should offer (which was accepted by the seller).

If a young boy who was discouraged can hear the voice of God, so can you. If unbelievers and kindergarteners can hear the voice of God, so can you. If people not even seeking God can have dreams, visions, and revelations of truth – hearing God's voice - how much more can those who seek Him hear Him? In reading this book, you are far better positioned to hear Him than you realize. Welcome to the new chapter of your walk with God!

2. I hear God more than I realize.

"My sheep hear My voice, and I know them, and they follow Me." (John 10:27)

"He who is of God, hears God's words." (See John 8:47)

Jesus said, "My sheep hear my voice." It wasn't sometimes. It wasn't perhaps. It wasn't maybe. It was a statement of truth. "They hear Me." So, if you are a follower of Jesus Christ, the Good Shepherd, then you can hear His voice whether you realize it or not. It's simply a part of who you are as a follower and child of God.

Jesus fully paid the price for everyone to be completely restored to a perfect relationship with God the Father. Every single one of us can hear God. The challenge is not that He is silent or that you can't hear; the challenge is that many of us are not yet aware that we hear God. Once we are tuned into the truth that we hear God, we discover that we hear Him much more than we previously realized. You have been hearing God more than you realize! Take a moment to say that to yourself. "I hear God more than I realize." It doesn't matter whether your mind agrees with you or not. It is true. It's like gravity. Whether you agree with gravity or not, it's going to happen. Regardless of whether you have a different opinion or lack of experience, whether the public media loves or doesn't love it, it will happen.

Often, how we hear God is so subtle we don't recognize that it is Him. Janine was preparing for a trip recently and had a random thought, "I should put my extra (eye) glasses in my bag." She didn't stop to fully recognize that it was God speaking to her. Thankfully, she did put extra glasses in her luggage. While we were traveling, her primary glasses broke, so she was very grateful that she had listened to God's Voice, even though she wasn't fully aware at the time that it was Him. The more we develop the 'muscle' of listening for God's voice, the more aware we are of how much He speaks and how easy it is to hear Him.

The inevitable truth is that you hear God more than you realize. Over these following few chapters, you will (re) discover how much He is speaking to you. You will grow stronger and stronger in your confidence and your ability to hear God's voice and to know that you are hearing Him.

As you continue to lean in and practice listening for God's voice, you will discover, "Oh wow! God is speaking more than I realized, and I'm learning to hear His voice more and more." Why? Because you are one of His sheep, and His sheep hear His voice. It's the truth. It's what Jesus, the Word of God, said, which settles it.

It's Probably God

Andy was deeply impacted by how much we hear from God through the teaching of author and speaker Dan McCollam. Andy grew up unconsciously believing that a big God was in the sky waiting for him to mess up so He could hit the imaginary 'exit' or 'punish' button over his life. Religion teaches that God is distant, angry, and indifferent, but this could not be further from the truth about our Father God, who represented Himself to us through the life of Jesus Christ. Religion teaches that you are not good enough to hear and that God is not kind enough to speak, so if you hear something, it's 'probably just you.' As a follower of Christ, this belief results in living like we have one foot on the accelerator and one foot on the brake because we are constantly second-guessing what we hear. We have the overly cautious, internal dialogue saying, "It might be God, but it's probably just me."

Dan McCollam's teaching opened the Scriptures, revealing that if you ask God for a Word, He will answer you.

> *"So I say to you, ask, and it will be given to you; seek, and you will find; knock, and it will be opened to you. For everyone who asks receives, and he who seeks finds, and to him who knocks it will be opened. If a son asks for bread from any father among you, will he give him a stone? Or if he asks for a fish, will he give him a serpent instead of a fish? Or if he asks for an egg, will he offer him a scorpion? If you then, being evil, know how to give good gifts to your children, how much more will your heavenly Father give the Holy Spirit to those who ask Him!"*
> *(Luke 11:9-13)*

We serve a good Father who wants to connect with His children. He wants to speak with you! So, when you come to God and ask Him to talk to you, He will. If you have a thought, an idea, a Scripture, a song, or an image come to mind, it's probably God. This takes your foot off the brake and puts it firmly on the accelerator of your relationship with God. Later chapters discuss how we may hear wrong ("it might be me") and what to do. But as we lay a foundation of hearing God's voice, we must first establish the truth that God speaks, and we hear more than we realize.

Stay Childlike

Another simple key to hearing God's voice is to stay childlike. Trust God like a child does. Andy was looking after a friend's son, who was about six years old, not yet smart enough to know the risks and the dangers of some things he did. He loved to climb up on top of a dresser and launch himself into

Andy's arms. The dresser was about three feet (one meter) tall. He would launch himself as far as possible, trusting that Andy would catch him. The game got to the point where he would face away from Andy and jump backward, trusting that Andy would catch him. He loved it. As this progressed, Andy grew nervous because if he hadn't paid complete attention, he could have unwittingly let the launching boy fall!

God is much more reliable and trustworthy than Andy! He knows every hair on our heads and has millions of good thoughts toward us! What if we fully trusted God and launched ourselves into His arms? He is completely reliable and always pays attention. He never sleeps! We can trust Him because though we may stumble, He will never let us crash to the ground; He holds us with His massive arms!

> *"The steps of a good man are ordered by the Lord, and He delights in his way. Though he fall, he shall not be utterly cast down; for the Lord upholds him with His hand." (Psalm 37:23-24)*

Staying childlike means to stop reasoning yourself out of what God is leading you into.

> *"Trust in the Lord with all your heart, and lean not on your own understanding; In all your ways acknowledge Him, and He shall direct your paths."* *(Proverbs 3:5-6)*

Stay childlike and in a place of taking risks. Lean into trusting Him and stepping out. Don't allow your 'smart' adult brain to reason you out of what you are hearing God say. Respond!

3. Listening increases hearing.

"For whoever has, to him more will be given, and he will have abundance; but whoever does not have, even what he has will be taken away from him."
(Matthew 13:12 NKJV)

The New Living translation puts it this way:

"To those who listen to my teaching, more understanding will be given, and they will have an abundance of knowledge. But for those who are not listening even what little understanding they have will be taken away from them." (Matthew 13:12 NLT)

"Incline your ear, and come to Me, hear and your soul shall live." (Isaiah 55:3a)

Have you ever had the experience where your spouse is talking to you while you are busy doing something, and suddenly you hear, "You're not listening to me!" It's incredible how much we don't hear when we are not fully listening. But if we pause, turn aside from what we are doing, and pay attention, we start to hear more of what is being said. Even more so, we communicate value to the one who is speaking.

Additionally, if we go into a conversation with a pre-determined expectation of what the other will say, we only hear what we want. But if we approach a conversation with genuine intent to listen and understand, what can happen is astounding. Our ability to hear increases, value is communicated, and connection grows.

The story of Moses illustrates this. Moses wandered the desert for 40 years, looking for something to feed his sheep. Then, one day, as he was tending to his responsibilities, he noticed a bush that was burning yet not being consumed.

"And the Angel of the Lord appeared to him in a flame of fire from the midst of a bush. So he looked, and behold, the bush was burning with fire, but the bush was not consumed. Then Moses said, 'I will now turn aside and see this great sight, why the bush does not burn.' So when the Lord saw that he turned aside to look, God called to him from the midst of the bush and said, 'Moses, Moses!' And he said, 'Here I am.'" (Exodus 3:2-4)

Notice that it was when Moses turned aside that God called to him. When we turn aside and put effort into listening, we increase our hearing. Our prayers have often become one-way conversations rather than interactions with the God who speaks back. We have an invitation to grow in our connection with God as we take time to turn aside, listen, and value what we hear.

When we (Andy and Janine) personally have time with God, both alone at home and in corporate settings, we each have a journal or device handy to write down what we believe we are hearing God say. Why? Because we want to value God's words for us. The Creator of the Universe is interacting with us; we don't want to take lightly or forget what He is saying. We want to value it and be able to go back and reread it rather than rushing on to the next thing. God's words have the power to change our lives.

"Then the Lord said to me, 'You have seen well, for I am ready to perform My word.'" (Jeremiah 1:12)

"So shall My word be that goes forth from My mouth; It shall not return Me void, But it shall accomplish what I please, and it shall prosper in the thing for which I sent it." (Isaiah 55:11)

When we talk to God, He listens, hears, and responds.

> "*Ask, and it will be given to you; seek, and you will find; knock, and it will be opened to you. For everyone who asks receives, and he who seeks finds, and to him who knocks it will be opened. Or what man is there among you who, if his son asks for bread, will give him a stone? Or if he asks for a fish, will he give him a serpent? If you then, being evil, know how to give good gifts to your children, how much more will your Father who is in heaven give good things to those who ask Him!*" (Matthew 7:7-11)

> "*Call to me, and I will answer you, and show you great and mighty things, which you do not know.*" (Jeremiah 33:3)

God, the Father of the Universe, wants to talk with you. His Word, the truth, makes it clear that He is always speaking, and all He needs from us is for us to turn aside and hear Him. Isaiah 65:24 says that before we can even call to Him, He is answering, and while we are still speaking, He hears. It's time to ask Him to help us listen and hear Him!

We have learned to turn aside regularly and ask Him to speak to us. We are led each day by His words, not just in Scripture but also in His freshly spoken words, which lead and guide us throughout life.

ACTIVATION:

Steps to Increase Hearing

The lies (whether ignorance or false beliefs) about God, ourselves, and life, hinder us from living fully in the way that God intended. As we practice hearing God, let us ask Him to uncover one lie that we believe stops us from living fully with Him.

> *"And you shall know the truth, and the truth shall make you free."* (John 8:32)

- Ask God: "What lie that I believe stops me from living in the fullness you have for me?"

- Pause and focus your mind and attention on Him. What do you sense He is saying to you? It could be that you 'hear' something, 'see' a picture, or perhaps you get an impression. It doesn't matter how you 'hear' Him, just that you pay attention to what you sense. Maybe you sense that He is saying you believe that you are not good enough. Perhaps you think that He only loves you if you are doing well. Remember, these are lies that hinder us.

- Give Jesus the lie you believed and ask Him to show/tell you the truth. "Jesus, I give you the lie that ... (state the lie you heard). What is the truth you give me?"

- Pause and listen to Him again as He tells you the truth. Meditate on the truth and turn this into a declaration for your day.

Step 1: Make declarations about hearing God

Read over these truth statements three times, saying them out loud at least once.

- I am a follower of Christ, and I hear His voice. (John 10:27)

- I hear God more than I realize.

- I am a child of God, and I know His voice well.

- It is easy to hear the Voice of God.

Step 2: Set aside regular time to hear God's voice

- Decide to include listening and hearing God in your daily time with Him.

- Read His Word (Scripture) and ask God questions about what you're reading. For example, ask, "Father God, what do you want me to know from this passage?"

- Pray - Talk to God and ask Him to answer you. Pause and listen for His response.

- Find a way that works for you to record what you hear Him say. Keep this nearby throughout your day to capture what you hear at any moment.

CHAPTER TWO:

Two Foundational Pillars

The planned end-use changed during the construction of a multi-story building in Korea. Workers were instructed to remove multiple support columns. The building was completed, and shortly after it opened, it was full of department store shoppers. However, removing the support columns subsequently led to widespread cracking in the roof when some heavy air conditioning units were moved. The owner refused to evacuate the building for fear of loss of revenue. Not long after, the building collapsed, killing 502 customers and injuring an additional 937[1].

The pillars and foundations on which we build our lives are a matter of life and death. Truth is the only foundation that never cracks or collapses. If we shortcut or attempt to alter our original design and remove structures that align and undergird us, we will inevitably end in ruin and loss—not just our own! Truth is non-negotiable for us to build our lives and communities safely and securely.

In this chapter, we outline two foundational pillars for a lifestyle of hearing God at work: the Word of God and wise counsel.

1. The Word of God.

Today's world tries to convince us that we can each have our version of 'truth,' but the bible clearly shows that only Jesus Christ and the Word of God provide us with the plumbline of truth.

"The entirety of Your word is truth, and every one of your righteous judgments endures forever."
(Psalm 119:160)

"Thomas said to Him, 'Lord, we do not know where You are going, and how can we know the way?' Jesus said to him, 'I am the way, the truth, and the life. No one comes to the Father except through Me.'" (John 14:5-6)

"And you shall know the truth, and the truth shall make you free." (John 8:32)

"Sanctify them by the truth, your word is truth."
(John 17:17)

As we grow in hearing God's voice, we want to build on the foundation of truth in the Word of God. We don't want to build on a faulty foundation that will leave our building vulnerable, with cracks or leaning to one side.

"For the Word of God is living and powerful, and sharper than any two-edged sword, piercing even to the division of soul and spirit, and of joints and marrow, and is a discerner of the thoughts and intents of the heart." (Hebrews 4:12)

The Bible is the Word of God and our daily anchor and guide. We read and immerse ourselves in it every day and intentionally allow it to shape and challenge how we see the world—the thinking and behavior toward all aspects of life.

We read to find courage and strength. We read to know the One in Whom we live and move and have our being. We don't just read to achieve a task on an imaginary list of spiritual disciplines; we read to commune with the Word and to let it change us. Jesus Christ is the Word of God (see John 1). So, when we read the Scriptures, we are communing with Jesus. His Word is the standard of truth for our lives. It shapes our values and beliefs. It challenges how we live. How can we know the truth if we are not anchored in something that does not change? The standard of truth that never changes is the Word of God.

A Quick Tip: Start With a Chapter of Proverbs Each Day

The whole Bible trains us on how to live. The best book of the Bible that gives focused wisdom for work is the Book of Proverbs. A wonderful thing about Proverbs is that it has thirty-one chapters, which aligns nicely with the fact that most months have thirty-one days. So, a quick start to getting anchored in the wisdom of the Word is to read one chapter of Proverbs each day—the chapter that aligns with that day of the month.

Don't limit your reading to the book of Proverbs. That would only give you one part of the equation, like knowing a person by studying only the right arm. The entire Bible is filled with insight, wisdom, and encouragement for life. We encourage you to read through the Bible because that will give you a complete understanding of God's name, nature, ways, and character. The more you know who He is through the Word, the more you can discern His voice in your daily decisions and circumstances.

Benefits of the Word of God as a Pillar in Your Life

Reading, meditating on, and letting the Word of God influence us have many specific benefits. Here are just a few:

- The Word of God helps us discern our thoughts and intents. It gets to the heart of our motives and allows us to see where we need His grace to change. Discernment is not just knowing the difference between right and wrong; it is knowing the difference between right and almost right (Charles Spurgeon).

  "For the Word of God is living and powerful, and sharper than any two-edged sword, piercing even to the division of soul and spirit, and of joints and marrow, and is a discerner of the thoughts and intents of the heart." (Hebrews 4:12)

- The Word of God teaches and corrects us. It teaches us how to live in a way that brings glory to God. It equips us for life. This means we can trust the process, knowing that we may not know much at first, but we will continue to grow and be equipped as we continue in the Word. As a result, we continue to get stronger, clearer, and truer as we build in life!

  "All Scripture is given by inspiration of God, and is profitable for doctrine, for reproof, for correction, for instruction in righteousness, that the man of God may be complete, thoroughly equipped for every good work." (2 Timothy 3:16-17)

- The Word of God helps us grow in faith. As we hear what the Word says to us and see the stories of the people who have gone before us, we are inspired to grow in our faith. This means we can find the confidence to move forward when faced with challenges, uncertainty, and transition.

"So then faith comes by hearing, and hearing by the Word of God." (Romans 10:17)

- The Word of God guides and shows us which way to walk. It directs us in our decision-making. As we bring our plans and thoughts and submit them to the Word of God, His truth will shine through, highlighting which way(s) to turn. This is a continual relationship more than a transactional yes or no. In later chapters, we give you multiple case studies, and the book "Finding Hope in Crazy Times" by Andy Mason contains 30 short chapters with a specific example (like a devotional) in each.

"Your Word is a lamp to my feet, and a light to my path." (Psalm 119:105)

- The Word of God protects us from error and allows us to know right from wrong. When we take the time to engage with it and interact with it in all the situations we face, we can trust that the God of His Word will keep us from being stupid!

"Your Word I have hidden in my heart, that I might not sin against you." (Psalm 119:11)

- His Words are spirit and life to us. They are the very lifeblood of believers. When we allow the Holy Spirit to speak through the Bible, it is life-giving and changes us.

"The Words that I speak to you they are Spirit and they are life." (John 6:63b)

Does What You Hear Line Up With Who He Is?

The Word of God becomes a pillar in our lives through daily reading, studying, and meditation (thinking on it), and allowing it to shape how we live. This is essential in hearing God at work. God will never speak something to you that contradicts who He is in Scripture. An obvious example is that He will never tell you to cheat on your taxes, steal someone else's product, or kill your pain-in-the-neck competitor. As you learn to hear the voice of God, test and align what you are hearing with the Word of God. Does what you hear line up with who He is?

Give the Holy Spirit Something to Work With

Knowing Scripture also allows the Holy Spirit to bring to memory certain verses that help us at any given moment. Perhaps you are having a difficult day and feel like something is impossible. The Holy Spirit may remind you that "...with God, nothing will be impossible" (see Luke 1:37). You may be faced with two good decisions and feel torn about which way to go. You are reminded, "Your ears shall hear a word behind you, saying, 'This is the way, walk in it,' whenever you turn to the right hand or whenever you turn to the left (Isaiah 30:21).

Recently, Andy was frustrated with a "lack of growth" (i.e., slower than desired) and questioned whether we should continue with some marketing initiatives to reach people with our message. Andy said, "I'm unsure if I'm called to the crowd." After a short dialogue with Janine, in which she challenged him to ask the Holy Spirit, Andy heard the Holy Spirit say (more like a command), "Call the crowd!" He was immediately reminded of a Scripture, "Surely you will call a nation you do not know, and nations who do not know you shall run to you, because of the Lord your God, and the Holy One of Israel; for He has glorified you" (Isaiah 55:5). This verse was one that Andy had memorized as a young adult... now over 20 years earlier!

As you learn to hear God and ask Him questions, He will remind you of what you have read in Scripture. The Holy Spirit will help you. The Holy Spirit takes the Word of God and makes it alive to you. As you read, you are not just reading for information; you are reading to let it come alive in you! You are inviting the God of all creation to commune with you. You are listening for the Words that seemingly light up on the page or in your spirit. This is the Greek word "Rhema" (see Strongs concordance G4487), which refers to the word of God. Rhema means the Word that God is currently speaking to you. It's the Word that jumps off the page at you as you read. Let Him talk to you through the Word!

2. Wise counsel.

The second pillar that provides alignment, support, and protection as we grow in hearing God's voice is wise counsel. Proverbs says, "Plans fail because of the lack of counselors, but with many counselors, they're established or succeed" (see Proverbs 11:14).

> *"Without counsel, plans go awry, but in the multitude of counselors they are established."* *(Proverbs 15:22)*

> *"A wise man will hear and increase learning, and a man of understanding will attain wise counsel."* *(Proverbs 1:5)*

> *"The way of a fool is right in his own eyes, but he who heeds counsel is wise." (Proverbs 12:15)*

We may hear the Word of God speaking to us and lean in to listen to His voice, but often, we are left with the question, "How do I apply that?" "What is the best timing?" and "What is the best approach?" We need discernment and wisdom to know what to do.

Intentionally processing what we are hearing with a wise counselor helps us know what to do with what we are hearing. Wise counselors can also 'bump' us back into proper alignment if (or when!) we start to veer off track. We need people around us who have the ability and courage to speak truth into our lives, even if it is not a fun conversation! Far too often, leaders only surround themselves with people who will tell them what they want to hear rather than those who dare to stand up and respectfully communicate a different opinion. It is imperative to have someone nearby who will tell us when we are hearing from our desires rather than the voice of God.

> *"For the time will come when they will not endure sound doctrine, but according to their own desires, because they have itching ears, they will heap up for themselves teachers; and they will turn their ears away from the truth, and be turned aside to fables." (2 Timothy 4:3-4)*

Wise or Critical?

As we started building Heaven in Business, we had a group of wise counselors, or advisors, around us. They were established in business. They were people of sound character. And they were successful in what they had built. One morning, we met with a wise counselor who pointed out everything we were doing wrong. It wasn't that we didn't know those things, and while it was somewhat helpful, we left the meeting feeling discouraged. We were thinking, "Oh no, are we ever going to get anywhere?" In the afternoon, we met with another one of our wise counselors. During this second meeting, the wise counselor pointed out the same things, but we left feeling encouraged and motivated. We felt like, "Wow, we can do this!"

What was the difference between those two wise counselors? The first counselor saw the problems and spoke only of the issues. The second counselor saw what needed attention yet spoke with encouragement and confidence that we could do this. This wise counselor took the extra time and heart posture to believe in us and speak with affirmation rather than just providing critical feedback.

When looking for wise counselors to speak into your life, look for someone with the wisdom to see what needs to be done and the ability to encourage you along the way. Don't just look for someone that will give you good information. Look for someone with a spirit of encouragement who has your best interests at heart. You often know what you need to do; you just need the courage to do it. You need a champion who will be honest with you and do so with love and compassion.

How to Recognize a Wise Counselor: Wrinkles and Body Scars!

We describe wise counselors as ones with wrinkles and body scars. We are looking for wrinkles: the *visible evidence* of a life long enough to gain wisdom. We are looking for someone who has experienced multiple seasons, cycles, and experiences and has grown through it all. We don't want to talk to a twenty-something about navigating a recession or a single person about how to form a healthy marriage. We seek someone with visible evidence of time-tested results in these areas of life.

Second, we look for body scars. Have they overcome any challenges? How many? For how long? Are they still smiling? What did they learn? If you have tremendous success in a booming economic cycle, it is not a result of your great wisdom! If you have consistent growth through multiple economic cycles, betrayal and lawsuits, changing consumer preferences, and more... then you have displayed some wisdom to learn from!

However, beware of the scar; not all scarred wise counselors are worthy of your attention. The key is, metaphorically, to know whether the scar is healthy (indicated by joy and generosity) or whether there is still a knife in the wound, and it is oozing offensive substances! If the wise counselor has wisdom to give but is cynical and still offended by what they have been through, stay far away!

How to Recognize a Wise Counselor: Romans 16:19, 20

Another test framework we use in identifying wise counselors is Romans 16:9. Paraphrased, this says, "Be excellent at what is good, and innocent of evil. And the God of peace will soon crush satan under your feet."

Excellent at what is good – does the wise counselor (and their company) have a sound reputation in the community for their work? Have they grown in excellence, or are they average? What makes them stand out? What do the reviews say?

Innocent of evil – does the wise counselor model godly character proven over time? How do they treat their spouse and employees, especially those lowest on the pay scale? How do they talk about authority and paying taxes?

In both tests, are there any adverse reports or concerns? Do not be naïve. Pay attention, as Jesus taught us, "Behold, I send you out as sheep in the midst of wolves. Therefore, be wise as serpents and harmless as doves" (Matthew 10:16). Many well-meaning believers have over-emphasized being as innocent or harmless as doves, forgetting we are equally commanded to be as wise and shrewd as serpents! Keep your eyes open. Don't simply trust someone just because they profess to be a Christian at work. Do your due diligence!

Crushing satan – when looking for a wise counselor, specifically in integrating faith and work, it is non-negotiable that they have current stories of their walk with God and of God working on their behalf in the workplace. The emphasis is on *current*. We all love the stories of the parting of the Red Sea and provision in the wilderness, but what is God saying today, and how did God show up on your behalf last week? Do not hesitate to ask these questions before you engage!

When our family heard God say to leave everything in New Zealand and come to the United States, we approached five different wise counselors to test if what we were hearing and applying was accurate. We didn't tell them all we heard. We started by saying we sensed God was speaking to us about a big transition. We asked them to pray about it and then come back to us with what they heard. Each one came back to us, and as we laid out all we thought we were hearing, they confirmed it and added the courage we needed to step out. We did the same when we sensed God say leave the West Coast of the United States and head to Pennsylvania. Today, we have a board of advisors that we regularly reach out to when we sense we are hearing God for a new direction or when we are feeling challenged. God made us part of a body, and we strengthen one another.

> *"For as we have many members in one body, but all the members do not have the same function, so we, being many, are one body in Christ, and individually members of one another." (Romans 12:4-5)*

Open Your Eyes to See the Wise Counselors All Around You

In addition to our semi-formal board of advisors, we have individuals around our life and business who are wise counselors. We approach different wise counselors (paid and free) on various matters depending on the subject. These include marriage counselors, spiritual directors, financial

25

advisors, legal advisors, gifted serial entrepreneurs, seasoned ministers, and more. We encourage you to find wise counselors wherever you are!

Andy was working remotely with a business owner whose company was growing rapidly, but he was experiencing relational conflict at the senior team level. The owner was also a friend of Andy's. After repeatedly hearing the owner complain about his team (and spending time in prayer on how to address the issue), Andy said, "Hey, I hear you blaming everyone else for all these things. But I believe the real issue is you. You are trying to build a significant business, but you've only ever run small-scale businesses. You need someone, in person, around you to mentor you, to give you wise counsel."

Due to the personal connection and strong personality involved, it was a tough conversation for Andy to have. He knew that the feedback may have resulted in an end to the relationship. However, the consequence of not saying something could be even worse. Will Andy love enough to speak the truth or protect himself by staying silent? Ford Taylor's book, "Relacional Leadership" frames this as follows: "I care about you more than I care about how you feel about me." If we genuinely care about those we lead, we will say something.

The conversation between Andy and the owner was initially not going well. However, Andy had come prepared with examples and enough clarity to support his words. Then God showed up. Andy said, "I had one of those moments where boldness and confidence came over me spontaneously. I can see now it was the spirit of God, but at the time, I was leaning into the conversation out of deep concern that my friend was being unwise. At that moment, I said to him, "Actually, close your eyes right now. God will show you a picture of somebody already in your life who will be your wise counselor."

Afterward, the owner told Andy that he didn't believe what he was saying, but he went ahead with it anyway. To his surprise, he closed his eyes and instantly saw a picture of a businessperson in his local church community... that he didn't like.

Now, pay attention here. You need people around you who are different from you. That means you may not feel comfortable with them. You may not feel warm and buzzing with excitement about what they have to say to you. But those people may have a skillset and wisdom to add to you that you need for yourself. Who do you have around you, different from you, that you could learn from?

Andy's conversation with the owner resulted in him approaching the businessperson God brought to mind the next day. The owner said, "Hey, I was wondering whether you'd be willing to walk with us as a company and mentor me. You've already succeeded in a significant business, and I need help." The businessperson responded, "It's so funny that you ask. Two years ago, God spoke to me about walking with you and your business, and I was waiting for you to ask!"

Two weeks later, after reviewing the financial documents, the brand-new wise counselor identified some critical issues. If these had not been immediately addressed, they would have resulted in the complete loss of the company. Wise counsel is crucial for your success.

You have wise counselors all around you right now, just waiting for you to ask for help. That could be through resources and book recommendations - a sure way to get wise counsel at a meager cost! But there are also people in your life who are seasoned, who have wrinkles, who have encouragement, that you can ask to walk with you and give you advice for a season. Perhaps it's a one-off meeting that gives you wisdom and direction. Maybe it's a life-changing relationship that has been waiting for years for you to ask!

ACTIVATION:

Foundational Pillars to Hearing God

We have identified two foundational pillars as we build a lifestyle of hearing God at work. We recommend both, but we know that the Word of God is the only absolute truth. Even if the most esteemed wise counselor suggests something opposite to Scripture, do not proceed. Line your life and all that you hear first with the pillar of the Word of God.

The second pillar is wise counsel. Knowing that something is lined up with truth is excellent, but knowing how to build helps us build with confidence, knowing our application of truth will succeed.

Step 1: Grow with the Word of God

"Give us this day our daily bread." (Matthew 6:11)

The stronger the pillar, the more weight it can handle. The more firmly connected to the pillar, the better you can withstand pressure, shaking, or conflict. We are constantly growing, so we strongly recommend planning to deepen your relationship with the Word of God by spending time in the Scriptures. Schedule consistent, daily time to read (or listen), meditate, and journal. Make a plan to let the Word of God become more than a task to complete; it is a relationship to grow. Start your day with what God says rather than the media, text, or emails!

- How can you increase your priority of relationship with the Word of God?

- How can you dialogue with Scripture to hear what God is saying?

- Consider journaling with questions and the thoughts that follow:

  - What did I read?

  - What does it mean (Then? Now?)

  - What verse impacted me? What was behind that?

  - What will I do differently today as a result?

See below for further resources to help you grow your relationship with the Word of God.

Step 2: Grow with wise counsel

Pray and ask the Lord to reveal who around you fits the criteria of a wise counselor. Are they willing and available to speak into your life? Can you take them for a coffee and ask them questions to learn from them?

- Who will you reach out to for wise counsel?

- Who is already in your life?

- Who can you intentionally ask to shape you?

Further Resources:

S.O.A.P scripture reading framework or more:

- Biblegateway.com/blog/2023/03/6-bible-study-methods-you-need-to-know-and-try/

- "Finding Hope in Crazy Times: Daily Stories of Hearing God through Scripture," by Andy Mason.

References:

1. Sampoong Department Store, Seoul, South Korea, 1995. Forneyvault.com/deadliest-structural-failures-all-time and Wikipedia

Three Keys to Know God Is Speaking

So far, we have established that everyone can hear God; we hear God more than we realize, and listening increases hearing. Then, we reinforced the two foundational pillars of hearing God's voice: the Word of God and wise counsel. As you implement a daily practice of engaging with the Word of God to hear His Voice and meeting with wise counselors to gain insight and apply what you hear, you will inevitably grow in how much you hear.

This leads us to another question: What if something I hear is not specifically in the Word of God? How can I know in my everyday life that what I hear is really from God? In this chapter, we will explore three keys that, if lined up, will give you confidence that what you hear is from Him.

When we set our hearts to hear from God, many thoughts may bounce around. Thoughts of what happened last week, the list of things we need to do today, and what we will eat for dinner can all appear on the 'screen' of our minds. Sometimes, it is hard to discern where what I am 'hearing' is coming from. Is it me? Is it the devil? Is it last night's dinner?

It's easy to know it's not God speaking if it goes against what is written in His Word. It's straightforward that the bible says, "Don't commit adultery," i.e., don't pursue in thought or deed someone else's spouse. However, there are a lot of other areas where the bible does not give absolute instructions. No chapter or verse covers whether you should pursue a business deal at a specific time. Neither does the Word of God tell you which person to hire, although it may give you clues about what to look for. So how can we know if the things not explicitly covered by the Word of God are really from God? Here are three key questions that have helped us and will help you also:

1. Does it release life?

"The words that I speak to you are spirit, and they are life." (John 6:63b)

Jesus spoke many things to his disciples. They didn't always understand what He was saying. Actually, they *often* didn't understand what He was saying! In John 6, Jesus was talking about being the bread of Heaven and that His people needed to eat His flesh and drink His blood to live forever (see John 6:51). Many of his disciples didn't understand what He was saying, got offended and stopped following Him (see John 6:66). Jesus turned to the 12 apostles and asked them if they wanted to leave also. Here's how Peter answered:

"Lord to whom shall we go? You have the words of eternal life. Also, we have come to believe and know that You are the Christ, the Son of the living God." (John 6:68)

In other words, Peter is saying, "Jesus, we don't fully understand what you are saying either, but where would we go? Although we don't understand, we know our hearts come alive when You speak. You are the only one whose words create life in us!"

When you hear something you sense is from God, does it release life? It may be scary, and it may not make sense, but if it is the voice of God, you will sense something like a stirring of your spirit – where your head may not understand, but your heart has a conviction that this is the path of life. This contrasts with a thought or idea that may sound logical, but nothing inside you registers life or conviction.

While living in Redding, California, one Sunday, our 15-year-old daughter came out of the church service, hopped in the van, and said, "I think our season here has ended." It was a shocking statement, given that she was thriving in all areas of life (contrasted with the previous year during the pandemic). That statement somehow stimulated a radical new pathway of thought for Andy. He got home and had a thought, "If we were to leave, where would we go?" We had lived in that city for over a decade and had zero plans for any other location. We had a community. We had a dream home. We were part of a wonderful church. It made no logical sense. But something was stirring...

As Andy sat and pondered, another thought popped, "Where are our existing clients?" He started to draw a map of the cities across the USA where our clients lived. The next thought was, "Where would be central?" Andy thought it was just his ideas and followed the thread. He drew lines between the cities with the time to drive or fly between each. It quickly became apparent that most of our clients were on the east coast of the USA – 3,000+ miles from where we lived at the time (we mostly met with them via online calls).

Looking at the map of interconnected lines, Andy could see that the central location between clients was between Philadelphia and Harrisburg, Pennsylvania. We didn't know anyone there. It was the middle of nowhere! But an excitement started to spark inside Andy, which scared him! "Oh no," he thought, "Is this me or God? Are you speaking to us about moving?"

The next moment, Andy had a thought that he knew was from God because it was so random. "Go back and read your prophetic word from 12 months ago." Andy knew instantly this applied to a specific word that was written down. He found it on his computer and read the first page. Nothing. Then he turned to the second page to see a paragraph that had a bunch of hand-written comments and names of people that, at the time, we thought it might apply to. Andy re-read it, "Heaven in Business is going to have a red pin on the east coast. It will be a key to unlocking the cities of Boston, Philadelphia, and New York..." Andy was overcome with emotion as he recognized, "This is the voice of God speaking right now!"

"I don't fully understand what You are saying, but I recognize that this entire conversation sparks life in me!"

That inspired statement and series of thoughts led to a remarkable journey of Heaven in Business, moving from the West Coast to the East Coast of the USA, and the rest is history. You can listen to the series of podcasts before, during, and after the move by going to the resource page: Heavenin-Business.com/HearingGod.

When God speaks, His word releases life. This gives you the energy to act on what He said. The opposite is also true. If it is not the voice of God, there is no spark of life in your spirit, just a good (or bad) idea in your head.

Note: This is not necessarily wrong; it could simply be your own idea rather than the voice of God.

Another point to note is that God's voice convicts us – or brings to light and compels a response (see John 16:8). Conviction motivates change. Condemnation, on the other hand, is a depressed feeling of failure or guilt. When God speaks, even His corrections bring life and the courage and ability to change. When the devil speaks, you feel condemned, like you can never make the grade. That's not God. God's voice releases life.

"The thief does not come except to steal, and to kill, and to destroy. I have come that they might have life and they may have it more abundantly."
(John 10:10)

Another excellent example of God's voice bringing life is in Luke 24:13-25. Picture this: you have been following Jesus for three years. You have walked with Him. You have eaten with Him. You have experienced miracles, signs, and wonders. You have heard Him speak to crowds and children and even storms! You recognized Jesus as the prophesied Messiah and were thrilled to be part of His new Kingdom on earth. Then, all your expectations and hopes came to a heart-wrenching crash as your Messiah was betrayed, captured, endured a false trial, and tortured to death.

Did you see it wrong? Did you hear wrong? What did you miss? What do you do now?!

Now, three days later, you heard that a couple of the women had gone to the tomb where Jesus was buried, and the body was gone! Then, a couple of angels approached them, saying Jesus was alive. What?! Other disciples had gone to the tomb to see for themselves, and it was true.

I don't understand. I'm confused. I don't know what to do. "Let's get out of here!"

That is the case with two of Jesus' disciples walking towards Emmaus, approximately seven miles west of Jerusalem. The two disciples were trying to process all that had happened. They were most likely scared, confused, and grief-stricken. Then Jesus Himself walks up and joins them on the way, except "Their eyes were restrained, and they did not know Him" (see Luke 24:16).

Jesus asks them what they are talking about and then pretends He wasn't aware of what had happened (to Himself)! He then gently corrects them according to the Scriptures (from Moses to the prophets) that spoke of the Messiah's suffering and entering glory.

We don't know how long Jesus walked and talked with them (average walking speed is three mph, so the total distance would have taken a little over two hours), but as they approached Emmaus, they insisted Jesus stay with them... still not knowing who Jesus was! After initially indicating He was going further, Jesus agreed to stay the night.

> *"Now it came to pass, as He sat at the table with them, that He took bread, blessed and broke it, and gave it to them. Then their eyes were opened and they knew Him; and He vanished from their sight. And they said to one another, 'Did not our heart burn within us while He talked with us on the road, and while He opened the Scriptures to us?'"*
> *(Luke 24:30-32)*

Wow! Amid the confusion, uncertainty, grief, and not recognizing Jesus at face value, they still recognized it was the voice of God that significantly moved their hearts.

What were some of the keys in the story? First, they needed to listen. Second, they needed to continue listening even when they could have gotten offended or angry. Third, they restrained Jesus: they were hospitable and wanted Him to stay longer. And finally, as they broke bread together and prayed, Jesus Himself opened their eyes to see and recognize who was right in front of them. The lightbulb moment happened as they reconciled what they were sensing on the inside, which was the very voice of the Messiah all along!

What is one way to know God is speaking? His words produce life! His words stir you and cause your heart to come alive. His words make your heart burn, even if you don't understand.

2. Does it carry peace?

"I will appoint peace as your governor and righteousness as your ruler." (Isaiah 60:17b GW)

"And let the peace of God rule in your hearts, to which also you were called in one body; and be thankful." (Colossians 3:15)

As a disciple of Jesus, the peace of God is the Spirit of Christ within us ruling in the 'control-center' of our being (see John 14:27, 33 and Ephesians 2:14-17). Jesus is the Prince of Peace (Isaiah 9:6).

We choose ("let") peace rule, or we choose the absence of peace.

The original word 'rule' means to arbitrate or govern. In Scripture, this is translated to umpire, to decide or determine, and to direct, control, or rule (see BlueLetterBible.org). The amplified version unpacks the verse even more, saying (paraphrased), "Let the soul harmony which comes from Christ act as an umpire continually in your hearts, deciding and settling with finality all the questions that arise in your mind."

So, the peace of God, by His Spirit within us, becomes our governor or decision-maker. The presence of peace confirms the decision is a 'yes,' and the absence of peace indicates 'no' or 'not now.' Another way of understanding a lack of peace in this context is to sense a hesitation or 'check' in your spirit.

When we allow the Prince of Peace to help us make decisions or guide us, we can be confident that we hear God's voice. Likewise, if we sense a hesitation, we should pay attention! How often have you sensed a hesitation about something, done it anyway because there was no logical explanation otherwise, and suffered the consequences?

Andy's background is in banking, finance, and agriculture. He was invited to be on the team of a startup company providing e-banking services to an unbanked (and unreached) people group in a particular nation.

Andy knew the founders of the company. He already had a favorable judgment of their character and competence, and he enjoyed the thought of working with them. On top of that, this opportunity matched Andy's technical background and heart for missions and transformation while offering an excellent long-term financial return. So, at the initial meeting, Andy said, "Okay, show me more." The founders then emailed Andy the PowerPoint presentation of the business pitch and strategic plan. As he was reading it, Andy was surprised by a deep sense of the presence of God. "There was this peace, and a sense of joy, and life. I felt excited and emotional! I was thinking, "Oh wow! This is a no-brainer. This is God. I'm going to do this!"

Andy spoke to his wife, Janine, and they did further due diligence on the parties involved and the business details. As Andy and Janine processed the proposal together, they agreed and felt peace. It worked financially, for time, and for Andy's competency. They confirmed with the founders and asked for the legal documents to proceed to the next stage of engagement.

The company sent through the papers to sign, which Andy read through as a formality with no identified issues or concerns. He then picked up a pen to sign, formally committing to work with the company. However, at the point of touching pen to paper, Andy had a strong sense of hesitation. All peace was gone. He felt frustrated, even slightly angry with God. "Are you kidding me? It makes sense to do this. We agree. I felt your peace through the process." Andy paused. Through years of learning to trust the Voice of God, he knew there was no way he would proceed as soon as the peace governor in his heart shifted to hesitation. Trust the leading of peace.

It is important to note that Andy never found out why. There was nothing about the people or company to be hesitant about, but for whatever reason, the Voice of God led Andy in a different direction (or time). Be careful not to try to conjure up some seeming logical reason or case when, at the core of it, you know the Voice of God is guiding you elsewhere. Andy, somewhat reluctantly and out of obedience to the Voice, called his friends and told them he loved what they were doing, but it wasn't for him at this time.

Years later, reflecting on this story, Andy still does not know why he was not to be involved. It could have been a distraction from other things that were his assignment. Perhaps it was to give you a great illustration of being governed by peace! Regardless, we continue to grow in following the Voice of God in all our decisions. We don't live by the business plan or proposal alone; we live by every word that comes from the mouth of God (see Matthew 4:4). Let peace be your governor!

We can't talk about hesitation as the absence of inner peace without talking about the possibility of a different kind of hesitation: the kind that comes from the presence of fear. When God asks you to do something outside your comfort zone, the hesitation may not be about whether God is speaking but a lack of confidence or doubt in your ability to act on it. This is compounded by negative self-talk like, "Who am I to do that? I'm not qualified?!" Or it could simply be that doing what He says is terrifying – like leaving everyone and everything you know and going to a new country! As you read through the case studies and stories in this book, it will become apparent that a certain measure of fear has surrounded many of the significant things we have heard from God. You will notice that testing we are hearing God, getting confirmation and clarification from wise counsel, and taking many small steps in obedience, are keys to moving forward in the face of fear. "Whenever I am afraid, I will trust you." (Psalm 56:3).

When Andy worked in banking, he was part of a district team of 12 from the same office. After a few years of increasing performance, his boss asked him why he avoided taking on team leadership roles. Andy took the feedback seriously and talked with his pastor (wise counselor) about what was happening. That discussion revealed to Andy that he was avoiding opportunities to lead because of fear of appearing to be self-promoting. He was reacting to the behavior of another team member (loud self-promotion) by doing the opposite (hiding). What Andy thought was being humble was a thinly veiled hesitation due to fear.

Andy promptly repented, apologized to his boss, and vulnerably said, "Whatever you ask me to lead, the answer is, 'yes.'" Shortly after that, Andy was asked to lead the weekly team meetings. Three months later he was promoted into a new *regional* leadership role. It is unlikely this would have happened if Andy had still been avoiding leading locally due to an undefined hesitation.

As we have grown in following God's voice, we have grown in recognizing the difference between an inner hesitation being the voice of God and a hesitation due to fear. At every stage of your spiritual maturity, it is best to involve wise counselors to test what you are sensing and give a different or confirming perspective.

3. Is it impossible to ignore?

*"O Lord, You induced me, and I was persuaded
You are stronger than I, and have prevailed. I am
in derision daily; everyone mocks me. For when I
spoke, I cried out; I shouted, 'Violence and plunder!'
Because the word of the Lord was made to me a
reproach and a derision daily.*

Then I said, 'I will not make mention of Him, nor speak anymore in His name.' But His Word was in my heart like a burning fire shut up in my bones; I was weary of holding it back, and I could not."
(Jeremiah 20:7-9)

Sometimes, when God speaks, you know it is His Voice and have a deep sense of expectation and excitement as you step out in obedience – His Word is a fire in your bones, compelling you to act! However, the outworking of our obedience doesn't always unfold the same as we expect. This is the story with Jeremiah.

Jeremiah was a national prophet to Judah around 626 BC until Jerusalem and Solomon's temple were destroyed in 586 BC. Jeremiah is often referred to as the "weeping prophet" due to his passionate expressions of grief over the stubbornness of his people and the consequences they were to face. His life was marked by great personal suffering, rejection by his people, and constant persecution for delivering God's messages of warning and the need for repentance.

In the first chapter of Jeremiah, we read of how God profoundly called this young man (approximately 17-20 years old) as a prophet to the nations! God spoke of what Jeremiah's role would be and touched his mouth, saying:

"Behold, I have put My words in your mouth. See, I have this day set you over the nations and over kingdoms, to root out and to pull down, to destroy and to throw down, to build and to plant."
(Jeremiah 1:9-10)

Wow. Imagine what that would have felt like. You just got personally picked for a leading role in God's plan for the world! I can only imagine it would have been awe-inspiring (and somewhat scary). And I imagine Jeremiah starting to dream of what would happen in alignment with God's word.

"I'm going to speak God's word to God's people, and they will turn back to him and be rebuilt as a godly nation. This is going to be awesome!"

Jeremiah went on to do precisely what God told him to do. He was obedient, he spoke up, he was faithful, and he was courageous.

And it unfolded the total opposite of what he expected. Not only did God's people resist and reject what Jeremiah said, they mocked him, beat and imprisoned him, and conspired to kill him!

After about 18 years of experiencing this, we get to chapter 20, where Jeremiah sees his work as futile and unproductive. He finally complains to God:

> *"O Lord you induced me, and I was persuaded; You are stronger than I, and have prevailed. I am in derision daily; everyone mocks me." (Jeremiah 20:7)*

In other words, Jeremiah says, "You persuaded and enticed me, God. You tricked me into doing this. And I allowed myself to be misled." He continues, "I don't want to do this. It's painful. It hurts. It's not fun!"

And then Jeremiah gets to verse nine, saying, "But if I followed through with this complaint and stopped doing what You said, I couldn't! Because Your word is like a fire, a fire shut up in my bones. I grow weary of holding it in. Indeed, I cannot."

Sometimes, hearing God and acting on what He says might not be desirable, pleasant, logical, or safe. It may look different from what you expect. But regardless of the way you look at it, you know it's just the right thing to do, and it is impossible to ignore. It's not about the result or lack of results; it's about obedience. It's about faith. It's about not drawing back but believing and persevering to the saving of the soul (see Hebrews 10:40).

When we first arrived in the USA from New Zealand, we had no income for three years. Andy was initially a student at a ministry school. Then, although invited on staff in a new department, there was no budget for salary, and even when that did eventuate, more was needed to cover the needs of our family of six fully. We had some additional income opportunities, which were also delayed due to visa status and issues beyond our control.

Andy had some business advisors during this season to help build Heaven in Business. One of them took him aside generously, saying, "Andy, we see your value. You're a great asset. You shouldn't be working for nothing. Come with us. We'll get you a business visa and set you up with a decent income so you can fully support your family." At that moment, Andy thought, "This is great; it's an answer to prayer. It's a no-brainer. Let's do this!" Then he turned to look at Janine, and she asked, "What does Jesus say about that?" Andy's heart sank, and he said, "Oh no. This is crazy! But we can't take up this offer of income." Deep down inside, we just knew there was something that God was doing, and it didn't involve being independent from the local church. It didn't make sense, and neither was it pleasant. But we had to trust God. We had a prophetic word (and a night dream) from God to stay connected where we were. Although it wasn't fun, His Word was impossible to ignore.

Years later, it is easy to say, "Andy, you made the right decision." But at the time, it was like Jeremiah: "I don't want to do this, but Your Word is like a fire shut up in my bones. It is impossible to ignore. I must obey, regardless of the outcome."

We all love it when God speaks, and everything lines up perfectly. You feel a spark or a release in your spirit, empowering you to act on what He says. You are reassured with the confirmation of His Presence and Peace. Scripture is singing in the harmony of alignment. Wise counsel resoundingly confirms the decision. You boldly act on what He says, which turns out beautifully.

Sometimes God speaks in ways that make no logical sense, and His words may be costly and counter-cultural. Yet His word is impossible for you to ignore, and your conscience and conviction compel you to act. And you must obey and trust the outcome to the One who holds all things in His hands and works all things together for good for those who love Him and are called according to His purposes (see Romans 8:28).

ACTIVATION:

Three Keys to Know God Is Speaking

We cannot emphasize enough the importance of immersing yourself in the Word of God daily and building healthy relationships with wise leaders whose greatest desire is that God's will be done. In this chapter, we highlighted three additional questions you can ask (initially of yourself) to determine if what you are hearing is really from God. These are:

1. Does it release life, or is there hopelessness or condemnation?

2. Does it carry peace, or do you have a hesitation?

3. Is it impossible to ignore?

Step 1: Consolidating what you know of God's voice

Take a moment to remember and reflect on a specific time when you can now confirm that God spoke to you.

Consider the following questions:

- What were you doing at the time?

- How did God speak to you?

- What did you sense or feel (physically, emotionally, spiritually)?

- Did you sense life or a release of energy when you experienced His Voice?

- How much did it resonate inside of you?

- Did you feel His peace confirming His Word?

- What was your conviction?

Write down a summary of how you know God spoke to you. Repeat this exercise as often as you want with other examples of (correctly) listening to the Voice of God.

Step 2: Learning to listen

Remember when you considered or moved towards doing something and felt a hesitation or 'check' in your spirit? Pay special attention if this was disconnected from logic or reason. For example, you wanted to hire a particular person who met all the criteria, but just before offering them the job, you sensed a hesitation without intellectually knowing why.

Note: If you ignored the hesitation and it turned out poorly, please don't beat up on yourself for getting it 'wrong.' Instead, use the experience to learn and improve your ability to do it right next time. Every situation is an opportunity to grow!

Consider the following questions:

- What were you doing at the time?

- What was the situation, opportunity, or location?

- What is your hesitation or someone else's?

- What happened as a result?

- What would you do differently?

- How can you develop a greater sensitivity or awareness of God in this way?

Step 3: What is God saying right now?

What decision(s) do you have in front of you right now? Reflect on what you sense God is already saying or ask the question right now: "Lord, I want to know your voice, leading and guiding me in all things. What do you want me to know about this situation?"

- Write down what you sense the Lord is saying

- How much does what you hear contribute to the quality of life?

- How much do you sense peace or hesitation?

- Is what you hear burning in your bones and impossible to ignore?

- How does this line up with Scripture?

- Who could add wise counsel to what you are hearing?

Practical Guide and Case Studies

CHAPTER FOUR:

Five-Step Framework for Everyday Decision-Making

"Give us this day our daily bread." (Matthew 6:11)

Hearing God is supposed to change how we live. God wants to interact with us in all areas of our lives and to give us wisdom and input. It is not just about us getting directions from our 'boss' on what to do. God didn't pay the ultimate price for a workforce; He did so to restore a family! It is a growing relationship where God partners with us in our everyday activities so that we live life more abundantly (see John 10:10). Even more so, it is through this interaction that we enjoy the most incredible privilege of humanity, which is fellowship with Him (see John 17:3). It is about growing in trust and communion with Him as we learn to hear His voice in all aspects of life.

The following framework is just that: a framework. It is not a one-size-fits-all way to live. It is a tool to help or guide us as we seek to hear God daily. The framework leads us through decision-making, from challenge or opportunity to action. In this chapter, we will outline the framework, work through a real-life example, and then set you up to do the same.

We use the framework to help focus our listening for the challenges or opportunities we face. This always results in action, whether that is a tiny step or a giant leap (listening without action is empty or "dead" faith – see James 2:20). After acting and experiencing what happens as a result, we can re-assess and walk through the framework again. Note that this is more about the journey with God than the outcome or lack thereof. Even if you 'mess up' on hearing God's voice while following this framework, you will continue to grow more and more connected to Him. So, keep walking!

"And we know that all things work together for good to those who love God, to those who are the called according to His purpose." (Romans 8:28)

FRAMEWORK:

1. Situation

Briefly describe your current factors affecting your current situation. What is your challenge or opportunity? What decision do you need to make?

2. Hearing

What are you hearing God say? What inspired Scripture stands out to you, or what did you read this morning? Write it down before trying to translate it into what it means.

3. Meaning

What does God mean by what He said to you? Often, what we hear needs to be 'translated' for it to become something practical that we can act on. Sometimes, it helps to ask yourself questions like, "If I fully trusted that God was speaking to me, what would this mean?" Or "If I approached this with a child-like attitude, what would it mean?" (See Mark 10:15.)

4. Wisdom

What does wise counsel add to the situation? Refer to the section on wise counsel in Chapter Two. How does a wise and mature counselor challenge or change your perspective, affecting timing, attitude, or approach?

5. Action

What are you going to do because of what you heard? What simple action step could you take today that aligns with what you are hearing God say? What could simple trust and obedience look like?

"...faith apart from [good] works is inactive and ineffective and worthless." (James 2:20)

What does this look like in real life? Below is an example of a challenging situation during the Covid pandemic. If you want more examples from our lives, you can find them in the book *"Finding Hope in Crazy Times: Daily Stories of Hearing God."*

EXAMPLE:
___

Cashflow Problem Due to External Factors

1. Our situation:

All in-person Heaven in Business events were canceled as California closed down because of the COVID-19 epidemic. This meant a loss of income of about forty thousand dollars over four months. Andy was freaking out, anxious about the lack of income, and worrying about what we were going to do. The government grants and loans offered to some businesses weren't available to us because of the structure of the entity we were part of. What do we do with our events? What do we do for income generation?

Note: One of the significant events to be canceled was a Heaven in Business Executive Retreat. These three-day events are highly interactive and experiential, including a beautiful mountaintop location, excellent meals together, and lots of hands-on ministry.

2. What I heard:

Andy's daily morning habit is to read Scripture to grow in connection with God and to learn God's nature and ways for whatever is going on (wisdom from above – *see* James 3:17). Andy's default is to read the book of Proverbs that matches with the day of the month and that day was the fourth. As he was reading Proverbs 4 in the New Living Translation, the word 'don't' caught his attention because it was repeated. It was repeated nine times out of the twenty-seven verses in the chapter.

Here are some of them:

Verse 2b	"Don't turn away from my instructions."
Verse 5b	"Don't forget my words or turn away from them."
Verse 6	"Don't turn your back on wisdom."
Verse 15	"Don't even think about it: don't go that way."
Verse 21	"Don't lose sight of them (my words)."
Verse 27	"Don't get sidetracked."

Andy sensed life in the word "don't," which brought him peace before he knew what God was saying. Andy sat back and meditated... "What are you saying, God?"

"Don't change the subject, don't leave the path, don't wander off track."

Then, he wrote the summary and the reference(s) in his journal.

"Don't change the subject."

3. What does it mean?

Andy knew that God was saying don't change the subject, but this didn't make sense considering the events that were (supposed) to be canceled. At that point, he was not sure what God meant! Andy continued to ponder this, thinking, "There is no way we can keep doing what we have been doing. What do you mean, God?"

Note: Andy didn't receive a straightforward answer, so he pondered it throughout the day, trusting that God would make it obvious.

"Trust in the Lord with all your heart and lean not on your own understanding, in all your ways acknowledge Him, and He shall direct your paths."
(Proverbs 3:5, 6)

4. What does wise counsel add?

Later in the day, Andy happened to have a call with a friend who is also a wise counselor. As they were talking and processing what each was facing and hearing God say, out of Andy's mouth came a statement, "It's not about changing the subject; it's about changing the delivery!" The conversation with a wise counselor had enabled Andy to suddenly realize he had combined doing the event with how he was doing the event. Andy had assumed that the subject (event) was the same as the delivery (in-person).

In hindsight, this sounds obvious, but for a very interactive, highly experiential event, it seemed impossible to do this any other way than in-person... and in-person was canceled. Could there be a different delivery? Would it be possible to deliver an online executive retreat?

5. What will you do?

Now, the possibilities started to open. Andy met with the Heaven in Business team and explored different ideas. He spoke to a friend leading online events for years and heard testimonies of God's actions, even through an online platform. Andy's perspective and beliefs were challenged, which opened his understanding of what could be possible through a virtual delivery system. Instead of believing that we had to be in the same room for people to experience the Presence of God, we realized that it could happen simultaneously, anywhere!

What Happened as a Result?

The Heaven in Business team assembled a three-day online retreat with twenty-five paying business leaders from across the USA (and beyond!) We had to think differently and adjust our expectations. We had to distill everything to its core components and then work out a way to deliver that in a virtual setting. It was challenging but also exciting. The event was sold out. More people wanted to come than we had planned for, and the people who did come had their expectations exceeded (and so did we!). After the event, guests told us they had forgotten it was virtual within five minutes. Others were in tears as they experienced God right in the room where they were sitting, looking at a screen! It worked! We didn't recover all our losses, but we started making progress. We realized that we could do this repeatedly and could serve people anywhere at any time. Suddenly, we had a new stream of income. Our eyes opened to new possibilities that hadn't even crossed our minds.

"Now to Him who is able to do exceedingly abundantly above all that we ask or think, according to the power that works in us, to Him [be] glory in the church by Christ Jesus to all generations, forever and ever. Amen." (Ephesians 3:20, 21)

Five-Step Framework for Decision-Making

Now it's your turn. Work through the following steps: listen to God's voice, engage with wise counsel, and act on what you hear.

Step 1: What is your situation?

What opportunities do you have in front of you? What decisions do you need to make? What challenges are you facing?

Step 2: What are you hearing God say?

What Scripture(s) or phrase(s) are you hearing? Maybe you don't have all the answers now, but what do you hear Him saying? Write it down.

Step 3: What does it mean?

Interact with the Lord over what you are hearing. Ask Him what it means. Ask Him to show you more. Meditate on what He is saying. Allow Him to speak to you about what you are sensing.

Step 4: What does wise counsel add?

Seek out wise counsel and the perspective they can add to your hearing. Ask them if they can see blind spots in your hearing/sensing.

Step 5: What will you do because of what you are hearing?

Make an action plan to respond to what God says. Today, I will...

BONUS: What happened, and what did you learn?

Take a moment at the end of your day to review. What did you sense God was saying today? How did you hear Him speak, and how did you know that was God? What happened as a result? How have you grown in the knowledge of hearing His voice? What would you do differently?

If nothing else, take a moment to express gratitude that we are God's children with whom He delights to be. Thank Him for His leading and guidance today, and ask Him what He wants you to know.

CHAPTER FIVE:

Case Study: Hearing God, Breaking Free of Limitations

Sometimes, God speaks to us about change, but our existing grid of understanding is limited, so we cannot grasp what He is leading us into. In this case study, we unpack a story of sensing God speak about change, wrestling through what that meant, and finally stepping into a new world of opportunity. Once again, pay attention to how God spoke or led, what we did to position ourselves to hear, and what was involved or required to follow His Voice into new opportunities. As you do this, consider the decisions you are facing yourself and how this could apply to listening to what God is saying.

What Was the Situation?

In 2008, Andy felt unsettled in his work and life roles. We lived in beautiful Hawkes Bay, New Zealand, and he worked as a relationship manager at a large agricultural bank. It was an excellent job with great benefits, but Andy felt restless. Janine also sensed that we were about to enter a season of change.

We were involved in a strong local church – from discipleship to board governance to missions. We had a close, trusted community and family nearby. There was no external reason why we should feel unsettled at all!

What Was God Saying?

However, we sensed something was about to change; we didn't know what. With all our church ministry and mission involvement, we wondered if that was where God was leading. So, Andy went to our senior pastor and said, "Our heart is to do more, and God is talking to us about change. We are openly included in the leadership succession plan. Before we explore alternative options, is your plan to offer us a staff role?" His immediate answer was, "No. Nothing is going to change here for at least three years." While that was a surprise, it was also clearly a closed door.

So, where else could God be leading? At the same time, an opportunity came up in Andy's work that would involve promotion into a new regional management role. He applied, was interviewed, and got the position! However, as the new role and responsibilities became clearer, Andy realized the travel would compete with family and ministry commitments. It didn't make sense.

God was stirring change, but the two obvious options were either impossible or an apparent diversion from our calling and assignment. "It's not a ministry expansion. It's not a business increase. So, what is it? God, what are you saying?!"

Note: God is not our servant. We are His. We serve at His pleasure. While we would love to have Him answer us in the moment, He does what He chooses every time. And often, we don't know why. This tests our hearts, and if we are willing to ask and keep asking and yielding to His timing and answer, we will have a response. The wait is worth it!

Andy went on a mission trip to Uganda about a month later with a close friend. It was the fifth trip to that nation, and the local organization had successfully implemented leadership development, an operational microfinance project, and a working orphan care program. In reviewing the progress, Andy sensed God was saying, "Your work here is finished."

Andy processed what he heard from God with his friend and talked about the sense of change back home, including the lack of clarity in both ministry and workplace. Andy's friend said as they spoke, "Have you asked God if He is leading you to a different geographic place?" Now, that was a new thought!

We never imagined that we would move geographically from where we lived in New Zealand. Within ten minutes, we had grandparents who were eager, trusted babysitters for our four small children. We had another set of grandparents less than two hours away. We had close friends, a strong community, and a growing influence in our city and nation. We had a dream house with zero debt. We had no plans to move in the foreseeable future. The thought of moving geographically from the most beautiful place on earth was entirely beyond our self-imposed line of limitation!

But God's perspective is way bigger than ours. He will lead you beyond the limitations on yourself, your company, and your ministry... beyond possible! If you will listen.

When Andy got home from the trip, he wrote a prayer in his journal, "God, is our future in this location?" A couple of days later, Andy read a bedtime story from an illustrated bible to our four-year-old son, Ben. Ben always chose adventures like David and Goliath or Daniel in the lion's den. This evening, Ben chose a different story. It was the story of Abraham (from Genesis 12). Andy read out loud, "Get out of your country, from your family to the land I am showing you." Andy paused, somewhat shocked because it was like he was reading the Voice of God to himself! Could God speak through a children's bible?!

We had a visiting speaker for a midweek meeting at our local church two days later. He opened the bible to Joshua chapter 1 and began to read (paraphrased), "Now arise, you and these people with you, and cross over the river Jordan, into the land of risk and promise." Andy sat bolt upright, suddenly paying a lot more attention! The speaker unpacked how the river Jordan had been the line of limitation set for the Israelites for forty years as they walked in circles in the desert. But now the season had changed, and they needed to cross over their line of limitations to step into what God had for them next.

In his journal, Andy wrote, "Is our future in this location?" Within four days, he had heard God say twice, "Leave your current location and limitations and go to a new location."

Andy didn't know he had an internal line of limitations a few weeks earlier: "I'm not leaving this geographic location. Why would anyone leave this beautiful, comfortable, fully provisioned location?" Now God was saying to let go, cross over, leave, move!

Please note: When making big decisions, never decide alone, especially if you are in a covenant marriage relationship. God had spoken to Andy, but what about Janine?

The following weekend, Janine walked around home and said a silent prayer, "God, you have spoken to Andy, but I need to hear from You also. What are you saying to me?" Before she could finish praying, a thought popped into her head: Jeremiah 3:14. That is not a commonly known verse, and Janine had no idea what it said! She sat down, opened her bible, and searched for the reference. She read it aloud as Andy listened, "...I will take you, one from a city and two from a family, and I will bring you to Zion. And I will give you shepherds according to My heart, who will feed you with knowledge and understanding." Janine simply started to weep as she didn't just hear the words, she *felt* the Spirit of God speaking.

What Does It Mean?

We knew God said, "Leave your location and go to a new geographic location." But He hadn't said where to or when. As we processed this together, we read back over the Scriptures, and very clearly, Joshua 1:1 says, "Now." So, we did know the timing. It was 'Now.' But where to God?

Note that the process of hearing God is not fixed or finite. Hearing God is about intimacy, not instruction. It is about an ongoing dialogue and relationship with Him that invites you closer to truly knowing Him – His Word, His ways, His Nature, and His Name.

> *"And this is eternal life, that they may know You, the only true God, and Jesus Christ whom You have sent." (John 17:3)*

So, as a couple, we prayed and processed together. That involved talking and asking one another, "If you could go anywhere, where would you go? What about this country? Why would you go there?" We interacted with what God said and asked more questions. We were leaning in to hear what else He had to say. We were looking for an internal witness or a "That's it!" from one another.

Notice here how some of the things we learned in previous chapters are at work in this situation. How do you know God's speaking? His Word releases life, His Word releases peace, and His Word is impossible to ignore; it's like a burning fire in our bones.

Over the next two weeks, we continued praying, processing, and asking, "Where?" Janine remembered a conference we had attended in Auckland, where the ministry of a pastor from California had significantly impacted us. His name was Bill Johnson, and he had mentioned that their church also had a ministry school. Suddenly, Janine asked, "What if we went to where Bill Johnson is in California?"

As she said that, it was like fireworks going off between us. California was never part of our plan, and attending ministry school did not register on our dream list. This was a long way across our line of limitations, but we sensed, "This is God!"

What Does Wise Counsel Add?

Our understanding is that God was saying to leave New Zealand, go to Redding, California, and attend a ministry school. And the timing was now (doing some quick research, the ministry school started in a few months). We needed to run this by wise counsel to test what we heard and add clarity and confirmation. One of the people we spoke with was a mature and trusted prophetic leader. We told her God was leading us into something significant, but we withheld all other details. We asked her to pray and return to us with what she heard.

Three days later, she returned to us saying, "I was praying for you and sense that you are going to make a big move, that it is now, and that you are going to sit under an apostolic leader like Bill Johnson." Boom! Confirmation number one.

Given the move's significance (and how scared Andy was), we sought the counsel of five different, mature, and trusted people. Every single one of them confirmed the decision, timing, and location. "This is God; you've got to go for it!"

What Will You Do?

Now, we needed to act on what we were hearing. So many details had to be organized, from applying and being accepted for the ministry school to putting in Andy's resignation at work, sorting out visas, putting our possessions into storage, renting out our house, finding accommodation and schools for the kids in California, saying goodbye to family and friends... all in six weeks. With ten suitcases, four children aged 2-8 years old, and a lot of uncertainty, we left small-town New Zealand, crossed our line of limitations, and landed in the United States of America!

We had an obvious word from God, confirmed by all our wise counsel. We had a lot of unknowing to navigate and a lot of trust in God to learn! And God proved faithful.

Paraphrased: "Every word of the Lord is tested, refined, and proven to be true. (See Proverbs 30:5)

Since crossing our line of limitations, we have discovered a new world of partnering with God. We survived three years with no income. We won the Diversity Immigrant Visa Program to fastrack USA green cards (and became citizens). We published books. We overcame debilitating health conditions. We launched leadership development and coaching programs. We bought and sold houses. We faced fear and lack. We navigated wildfires and snowstorms. We saw physical and financial miracles. We made new friends all over the world – from Russia to Singapore to Guatemala to Zimbabwe. We started a movement connecting, training, and activating people to partner with God in all of life. We got to write this with you in mind!

What's the point? Now, we can look back and say, "Oh, it was obvious that God was speaking." But at the time, it required faith—faith to navigate the uncertainty and the unknown, faith to cross the line of limitations we had set for ourselves.

How did it start? We asked a question. We didn't even know what question to ask. We had a friend – a wise counselor - who gave us a different perspective and a question to pray about.

So, what about you? What did you observe as you read this small part of our story? How did we hear God speaking? What did we do to position ourselves to hear? How did we continue to understand what God said even when it didn't make sense? How did our line of limitations blind us? What was needed to see and hear beyond our 'no-go' zone?

Pause for a moment and ask, "Jesus, are there any lines of limitation that I (or others) have set for myself? What is the future that you have planned for me? How can I cross over my line of limitations and step into the land of risk and promise you are inviting me into?

ACTIVATION:

Hearing God and Breaking Free of Limitations

- As you reflect on the case study, what stood out to you? What does the Lord want to highlight for you in this case study?

- What did you learn for yourself? What will you do as a result of that learning?

Things to note from the case study:

- The journey started with a friend pointing out Andy's line of limitation. Before this, Andy hadn't considered the possibility of leaving our geographic location. Andy began to hear God more when he broke out of the limited thinking of his existing circle of influence. What line of limitation is stopping you from moving forward? Ask God to reveal this to you. What does God want to say to you about that?

- It was a significant decision for the Mason family. Andy and Janine both heard from God and processed the move together. Are there other stakeholders that will be affected or involved in what God is saying to you? Have you invited them into the process? What are they hearing?

- Have you sought wise counsel on the decisions you are making? Do you have people in your life to give input into major decisions or to help you see your lines of limitation?

- God may not be moving you halfway across the world now, but He is always taking us on a journey beyond where we are comfortable. Where is God inviting you to go beyond your comfort zone? Ask Him to show you. What will you do to accept this invitation?

CHAPTER SIX:

Case Study: Hearing God for a Business Launch

God wants to meet you wherever you are in your life and business journey. He has Divine 'set-ups' for you and is committed to your growth. He knows more about your life and business than you do and has ideas just waiting for you to discover... if you are willing to listen. In this case study, we unpack how God 'interrupted' Andy and the resulting launch of a business model that was not even a vague consideration moments earlier. Pay attention to what Andy did to set himself up to hear, what he needed to let go of, and what work would be required to partner with God in a business model entirely outside Andy's background experience.

> "For we are His workmanship, created in Christ Jesus for good works, which God prepared beforehand that we should walk in them." (Ephesians 2:10)

God knows where you are going and the good works He has called you to. He talks to us to get our attention so that we can get on the path to those good works. In this case study, we will use the framework presented in the previous chapter to demonstrate the process.

What Was the Situation?

About a year after arriving in the USA, Andy launched (what we eventually called) Heaven in Business, a local initiative experimenting with what is possible when we partner with the Presence and power of God at work. This rapidly grew to include a curriculum for students in the ministry school, an in-person executive retreat, and an annual conference. Results (testimonies) started to pour in. It was working! Everything was being delivered face-to-face, and the connections and momentum were growing. We formulated a vision for connecting, training, and activating one million businesspeople worldwide, partnering with God in their place of work and engaging in the well-being of the city they served.

However, we had a challenge. As Andy said, "I was limited to my time. I was limited in what I could do. I sensed God saying to be a catalyst and not to build a big organization. But how do you stay small and catalytic, limited to your physical time and capacity, and still reach a million people worldwide? That was going to take decades!"

Andy was stuck. Not only was he limited to the physical time of in-person meetings, but he was also limited by his beliefs about himself and his narrow business experiences. To give some context, Andy left school at the end of his junior year (17 years old) to train as a rancher - a shepherd. The on-site training program was a large ranch in New Zealand with 12,000 sheep, 500 cattle, horses and dogs, and 20 cadets (or trainees). Despite a subsequent business degree and a decade of agricultural business consulting, Andy still saw himself as a small-town country boy. Yet God said, "Andy, I'm calling you to lead a global movement of businesspeople who are partnering with God in their place of work."

Our self-determined view of ourselves limits us. It ties us up and stops us from becoming who God has called us to be. Consequently, we are blind to the potential God-strategy because we look at ourselves and see through the lens of our limitations. We can't comprehend the way forward because of our unbelief.

So, what can you do to change? It's always wrapped up in seeking first the Kingdom of God and His operating system (His way of doing things – see Matthew 6:33). Andy asked, "God, how do we grow? How do we achieve this vision? How do we do this the way that you are directing?" And then God spoke with the way forward. And it was not as expected. Sometimes, the unusual way God speaks causes us to think outside our limitations, and suddenly, ideas, opportunities, and strategies are multiplied.

"For with God, nothing will be impossible." (Luke 1:37)

What Did We Hear?

Andy woke early one morning after wrestling with how to grow and not having any solutions (he could see). He was supposed to go hiking with a friend, Matthew, at 7 am. When Andy woke at 5 am, he was lying in bed and had a random thought, "Don't go with Matthew." Andy wasn't fully awake and convinced himself, "That's just me." So, he rolled over and went back to sleep for another hour. On getting up at 6 am, "Don't go with Matthew" echoed in his head. He couldn't shake it, but it didn't make logical sense.

Andy started to reason with himself. "Why shouldn't I go with Matthew? That's strange. Maybe it's not God. Maybe Matthew should come with me in my vehicle instead of me going with him. Is he going to crash? Is his car going to break down? Is something going to happen? Maybe we should go somewhere other than where he suggested..."

This is all earthly reasoning, where Andy is trying to figure out what God is saying and why He is saying it. It is *never* a good strategy to try to reason with God! Trust in the Lord and lean not on your own understanding (see Proverbs 3:5). The best approach is to surrender your 'right' to understand, humble yourself, listen, and obey.

Finally, Andy said to himself, "If I was just childlike... if I simply trusted God at his Word... then I don't *need* to know why. I make the decision: I won't go with Matthew."

Andy promptly texted his friend, saying, "Hey, something's come up, and I can't go this morning. Sorry. Let's reschedule." Note: Andy did not tell his friend, "God told me not to go with you." This would have created unnecessary pressure and concern and misrepresented what God wanted to communicate to Andy.

Once Andy had made that decision, he opened his Bible and happened to be reading the book of Acts, chapters 15 and 16. This is the story of God sending the apostle Paul to the area of modern-day Turkey to preach the gospel and encourage the disciples. He got there and went to western Turkey, but the Holy Spirit forbade him from preaching the gospel there (see Acts 16:6). So, Paul changed plans and attempted to go to northern Turkey. Still, again, the Holy Spirit prevented him (see Acts 16:7). Paul couldn't preach in the west or the north, so passing by some cities, he came south to Troas and went to bed! That night, he had a vision of a man in Macedonia pleading with him to "Come and help us."

As Andy pondered the phrase "Don't go with Matthew" and the story of Paul being redirected ("Don't go there... don't go there... come over here"), he realized God was speaking about a change in direction. God wanted to direct us somewhere different from where we were currently headed.

What Does It Mean?

Andy had no idea what this meant but figured God was about to speak some more. This felt significant! His thoughts turned to the last time God spoke about a substantial change in direction: leaving New Zealand and moving to the USA. Was God redirecting Andy and Janine to a new location?! "What is the new location? Where is God telling us to go?"

With his brain still whirring, Andy drove to his office, closed the door, and sat at his desk. He closed his eyes and said, "Okay, God, I'm ready. Where do you want us to go?" Andy said, "Instantly, it was like something hit me in the chest. It felt significant. It wasn't God's audible voice but a loud internal voice, almost jarring. It wasn't just like a light bulb going off; it was more like a hammer." The phrase he heard was, "Go online!"

Andy was expecting a location... like Alaska or England. God said, "Go online." Was that even a location? The context was Heaven in Business and its growth. Andy knew nothing about an online business as a shepherd from New Zealand. But the voice of God was so clear and convincing that it was obvious. Andy just didn't know how.

What Does Wise Counsel Add?

Thankfully, Andy knew some people who knew about online businesses. Andy phoned the Director of Bethel Media (Bethel. TV) and received excellent advice about online business models, including some suggestions for reading to learn more. He then spoke with the people building Bethel Worship. They had just set up WorshipU.com, an online learning platform.

Next, Andy spoke to a wise counselor in the marketing space. He suggested talking with a copywriter and suggested two names. Andy pursued one with a much more professional online presence (RayEdwards.com). Andy emailed Ray, saying, "Hi Ray, [mutual friend and professional contact] referred me to you. I'm looking at launching an online platform, and I'd love your input and suggestions about how we could communicate what we do."

Ray responded, "I'm not taking on any new clients, and it will cost you much more than you can afford. However, you coached my son through Bethel's School of Ministry, so let's talk." Wow! Andy had no idea of that connection... and favor. You never know how the unconditional generosity of time or service today will benefit you in the future.

The subsequent conversation resulted in Andy sending Ray samples of our content and a copy of God with You at Work, which had just been published. We had set up another time to talk, but Ray phoned me ahead of time and said, "Andy, the Holy Spirit woke me up in the night to listen to your content and read your book. What you don't know is that I have Parkinson's. But when I listened to your content and read your book, my Parkinson's symptoms reduced to zero. Whatever you want to do, I'm in!"

God knows so, so much more about you than you do. He knows where you are headed and can set things up for you to discover along the way. When you look for it, you will find His fingerprints everywhere.

> *"You've gone into my future to prepare the way, and in kindness you follow behind me to spare me from the harm of my past." (Psalm 139:5 TPT)*

What Action Did We Take?

Following wise counsel, market research, and much learning, Andy put together a business proposal and started to move forward with the Heaven in Business online learning community.

Another significant step was raising $100,000 to fully fund the launch. Andy was initially going to do this slower, with a lower budget, from cash flow. But again, wise counsel challenged him to act as if he fully believed God was with him. "What would you need to employ someone and launch this straight away? What if you got ten of your business leaders to each contribute $10,000?"

Again, this challenged Andy's belief (fear vs. trust) system and pushed his vulnerabilities around asking people for investment. To put it plainly, Andy had a clear vision and plan but lacked confidence pitching this to his business community because he hadn't done this before and was afraid of losing support (which had never been tested anyway!). He was procrastinating. Andy put the pitch together and decided to practice by presenting it to the students in the school of ministry class he was teaching on Heaven in Business. In Andy's mind, it was safe. This was not the ultimate audience; this was simply practice and an excellent opportunity to involve the students in the learning process.

The pitch went well. Andy outlined the business proposal, the current and forecast impact and results, and what God was already doing through this new initiative. He presented how they would fund it: ten founding members contributing $10,000 each. Andy then took questions and feedback.

As the class ended, one of the students walked up. The retired Silicon Valley executive said, "Andy, I want to be one of your founding members." Next, an international businesswoman who happened to be auditing the class that day approached, saying, "I also want to be a founding member."

As Andy continued to have private 'feedback' conversations, people started sharing the pitch, and within a couple of weeks, he had confirmed $70,000 without 'officially' asking anyone! He intentionally approached one business, inviting them to be a founding member, and they declined. They didn't want to be an individual founding member; they wanted to join as a company with $20,000!

What's the point? The Heaven in Business team had a vision without a clear, implementable strategy. Then we heard God say, "Go online." He meant what He said: launch an online version of what you teach in person and multiply your reach worldwide. Andy had no experience in this and didn't know what to do. That was where wise counsel turned a good idea into a proven process... with a much bigger and better step towards execution—total funding!

As you lean in, ask for advice, and then sift the wise advice with the direction you hear from God, He establishes your steps. Once you know what to do, you still need to step out and trust Him. When we did that, God had more people waiting in the background, ready to help us more than we imagined.

God is your ultimate business partner. You can have Him as a silent partner or lean in, listen to Him, and get fresh strategy daily. When you do, you will discover He has already set up the things you need to move forward.

> *"For since the beginning of the world Men have not heard nor perceived by the ear, nor has the eye seen any God besides You, who acts on behalf of the one who waits for Him." (Isaiah 64:4)*

ACTIVATION:
***

Hearing God for a Business Launch

- What stands out as you reflect on the case study/ testimony? What does God want to highlight for you in this case study?

- What did you learn for yourself? What actions will you take as a result of that learning?

Things to note from the story:

- How did Andy hear God? How did Andy position himself to hear, and in what way did God speak? How did he respond?

- Simple obedience (not going for a hike) led to God speaking to Andy more. How can you turn aside to hear more? Where do you need to be obedient?

- When Andy turned aside and continued to lean in, he heard more from God. It was an ongoing conversation that led to "Go online." What does God want to discuss with you? How will you make time to listen to Him?

- Andy sought wise counsel. What He heard from God was well outside his comfort zone, in an area where he felt ill-equipped. Where is God leading you that you feel unqualified for?

- How did God meet Andy when he stepped outside his comfort zone in response to what he heard? Where have you seen God's faithfulness as you have stepped out in the past? Where is He asking you to step out of your comfort zone now?

Prayer:

Lord, I thank you for always speaking to me. I thank you that I am one of your sheep, so I always hear your voice. Please increase my awareness of your voice. Help me to respond to you and to turn aside in simple obedience. Thank you, Lord, that you go before me and you have people around me to help me. Thank you for always being with me. Let the knowledge of your Presence give me the courage to step into the unknown as I partner with you in all of life. Amen.

CHAPTER SEVEN:

Case Study: Hearing God for an Income Challenge

Most of us have experienced a time when our income was insufficient to cover expenses. What do you do when you don't have enough? How do you position yourself for more? What does God have to say about that? This case study is about hearing God for an income challenge. First, let us establish a belief framework for dealing with daily challenges:

> *"Man shall not live by bread alone, but by every word of God." (Matthew 4:4)*

Physical food, water, and oxygen are not the only things that sustain or give us life; we don't live by bread alone. Likewise, we don't live solely by the amount of money in our bank account, the level of our income, what the government is doing, or the condition of the global economy. We live by the Word of God - the freshly spoken rhema Word of God that gives life to the dead and calls things that do not exist as though they did (see Romans 4:17). If we want the results of listening to *that*

Word, then we need to have a daily lifestyle of prioritizing time to listen and respond to that Word. So, what are you reading and feeding yourself on each day? Are you seeking the Word of God first, or are you more invested in the fresh word from your favorite news source, podcast, friend, or social media feed?

"Give us day by day our daily bread." (Luke 11:3)

Bread is physical food and refers to God's freshly spoken rhema Word. Jesus taught us to pray to the Father, "Give us this day our daily bread." The emphasis is today and daily. It is today's bread, not yesterday's leftovers. It is fresh bread daily! And it is not someone else's bread; it is *our* bread. God has something fresh for us to 'eat' each day, and it doesn't come by taking what someone else is hearing. So, what does God want to say to you *today* to sustain, provide, and protect you *today*?

What Was the Situation?

When we lived in Redding, California, Andy received a salary from being on staff at Bethel Church (leading the business department called Heaven in Business). We supplemented that income through speaker fees Andy received from traveling about one weekend a month. With the global pandemic of 2020, all travel ceased, and a necessary component of our family cash flow ceased as well, resulting in an income challenge.

What Did We Hear?

Andy's daily discipline starts with reading Scripture. This season, he leaned in to gain God's solution for our situation. One day, Andy was reading Proverbs chapter thirteen, and a couple of verses stood out:

"A wise child accepts a parent's discipline; a mocker refuses to listen to correction." (Proverbs 13:1 NLT)

"People who despise advice are asking for trouble; those who respect a command will succeed." (Proverbs 13:13 NLT)

What Does It Mean?

A parent can refer to a community elder or wise counselor. One of Andy's wise counselors and friend is Ray Edwards, a highly regarded communications strategist and copywriter. The day before reading Proverbs 13, Andy had received an email from Ray saying, "I keep thinking about you. Let's have a conversation. I've got something to talk to you about." It just so happened that Andy and Ray were about to have that conversation on this very day, and God seemed to be saying, "You are about to get some correction or advice, so pay attention!"

To give more context, Andy and Janine had been discussing offering an online course as an alternative to travel (we had not done this before). We were talking about what price we should charge and were thinking of the $90-$150 range. Suddenly, out of Andy's mouth came, "I think we should charge $300." Andy agreed logically with what he said but was also scared of charging that amount because it sounded high, and he wasn't sure if the course was worth it.

Note: The core of this was not simply a question of the value of the course but a hidden self-doubt around the value he was contributing. "Am I enough? Am I contributing something of value?"

As we continued talking, Andy looked out the window and saw the first hummingbird of the season. Some cultures believe that hummingbirds are a symbol of favor. Others think they are a sign that God is sending you a message. Either way, to Andy, it was yet another reminder to tune his ear into what God was saying, especially what He was about to say, through his wise counselor, Ray Edwards.

What Does Wise Counsel Add?

On jumping on the call with Ray, the conversation turned to, "Andy, I was thinking about you. Whenever I have a conversation with you, I walk away with things that have changed my life. I think, wow, I need to pay you for this. We need to have an exchange of value. But then it feels weird and awkward. It's like there's something that's blocking you from charging, from asking for things that you need. What is going on inside of you?"

This was a setup! With all that God was speaking before the call, Andy was ready to pay attention and listen. Ray was speaking correction and offering some discipline that would result in success (see Proverbs 13:1,13).

Andy needed help with value. This translated to his uncertainty around product pricing. We had an income problem. The conversation with Ray was a perfect setup for God to bring adjustment to Andy's core identity (value) and, subsequently, the confidence to increase pricing.

Andy responded to Ray, "Okay, walk me through some things we can do." Ray immediately recommended *The Prosperous Coach* by Steve Chandler and Rich Litvin. He showed Andy a copy. On the front of the book was a hummingbird! Once again, this got Andy's attention.

Andy ordered a copy, and *The Prosperous Coach* arrived a few days later. The book is about more than how to coach; it is about the business of coaching and the belief to do this well! It references the hummingbird:

> *"The tiny, versatile hummingbird symbolizes the message of this book. A hummingbird's wings beat up to eighty times per second. They can rotate in a complete circle, allowing it to hover in mid-air, fly forwards, backward, up, down, sideways, and even upside-down.*

The laws of physics say it should be impossible for the hummingbird to fly.

Clearly, nobody told the hummingbird.

We dedicate this book to those of you who are ready to do the impossible."

What's the point? God sent a message, and it was loud! We thought we had an income problem. The truth is we had a belief problem. God spoke through Scripture, Andy's words, nature, wise counsel, and a book. As Andy read through the book, it gave language to what was happening and began to change his thinking from the inside out.

What Did We Do?

We acted on the advice and launched the course at a higher price (see HeyGodWhatNow.com). This turned into multiple online courses, and participants asked for follow-up individual and group coaching. The course became the foundation of the book you are now reading! The growth in individual and group coaching became a core business model and quickly exceeded the income from travel. Better yet, the coaching could be done literally from anywhere! Without knowing, this would make it financially possible to expand Heaven in Business from Redding, California, to Pennsylvania two years later!

God is so good. He knows your situation. He knows what you are walking through and has excellent solutions for you. He can speak through nature. He can speak through people. He can talk through books. God can use anything to help you hear what you need to hear. Are you listening?

ACTIVATION:
_____

Hearing God for an Income Challenge

- As you reflect on the case study, what catches your attention?

- How many ways did God speak? What did Andy do to prepare himself to hear?

- Andy thought he had an income problem, but it was a belief problem. Do you have any external challenge that is a belief issue God wants to adjust?

- What internal and external work would have been required to apply what Andy heard?

- What is God trying to tell you through this story? What will you do about that?

Things to note from the case study:

- Andy read the Word daily and leaned in to hear God's solutions to his situation. How much do you value hearing God's solutions to your problems? What would your schedule and attention say? What do you want to do differently?

- When Andy read about receiving correction from a 'parent,' he ensured his heart was open to listening and responding. Do you have a heart ready to receive from those God has placed around you? Who is God using to speak to you? Are you listening? Who have you invited to speak into your life?

- Andy paid attention to the hummingbird's 'coincidence.' This continued to catch his attention and was a message—do the impossible! What 'natural' things have you overlooked that God wants to speak through? What is He saying to you?

- Andy was recommended a book that addressed his issue. He had to read it to receive its wisdom. What have you been given access to or been invited to do that you haven't followed through on? What wisdom are you ignoring because of this?

- Andy had to adjust his business practices to achieve different financial results. It was not comfortable or easy, but it was necessary. What is God speaking to you about that is outside your comfort zone? How can you get help or take a small step in obedience to grow?

CHAPTER EIGHT:

Hearing God Through Our Filters

We all have filters through which we hear. We often don't listen to what a friend, teacher, leader, or boss says because we hear what we want to hear or translate what they may say through our experience. Another metaphor for this is a lens that we look through that gives us a filtered view of the world. How we grew up, our different cultural backgrounds, our experiences (or inexperience), and the conscious or unconscious training we receive all affect how we see the world. The good news is that God's ability to communicate is more powerful than our filters, and although we need to be aware of the effect our filters can have on us, God can speak to us despite them. If your heart is open to pursuing God and hearing His voice, He will adjust and shape you. He will refine you and grow you through the process. He works all things together for good, so you can trust Him!

Let's experiment. In a moment, you will read a word that will evoke specific memories or have certain associations for you. Those will be different depending on what you have experienced in your life. When you read the word, be aware of the thoughts, images, and emotions that arise.

The word is "missionary." What does this word mean to you? What are the images that spring to mind? Are there memories associated with that word? What emotions do you feel?

For many of us who grew up in a Western country, the most common image associated with the word 'missionary' is an individual feeding orphans in Africa or Asia. Perhaps this image reminds you of a mission trip you took as a teenager and all the memories that came with it. But is this the only definition of 'missionary'?

When Andy was thirteen, a visiting, traditional missionary spoke at church. His mother clearly remembers Andy saying after the service, "God told me to study agricultural science because I'm going to be a missionary and help people practically as well as spiritually." Ten years later, Andy completed an Agricultural Science degree focused on business management and international community development. He wanted to work for a company like Opportunity International or World Vision but needed more practical experience. So, he got a job in New Zealand as an agricultural business consultant and then in agricultural finance, helping rural customers achieve their goals. Andy still thought he would one day go to Africa and help spiritually and practically with his farming business knowledge.

Twelve years later, we heard God say to leave New Zealand and go to the USA, and our journey took a different turn as we completed a ministry school and launched Heaven in Business. At some point in this process, Andy realized that he is doing today exactly what God spoke to him about as a thirteen-year-old (now more than 25 years ago!) It just looks very different from what Andy imagined as a 'missionary.' Andy thought he would be in the dust, helping people experiencing poverty grow better crops and teaching them about Jesus. Instead, he is in conference rooms and board rooms worldwide, talking to 'orphans in suits' about their true identity with God and how to grow business that advances the Kingdom everywhere. What is Andy doing today? He is a missionary, helping people practically as well as spiritually.

If Andy had dogmatically stuck to his limited definition of missionary, would he be doing what he is doing today? And would you be reading this book?!

A friend was invited to start a ministry school in southern Africa. It seemed like a dream come true for him, and he couldn't wait to be a 'missionary.' In the process of preparation, he fell in love with an American businesswoman. He thought, "Wow, we're going to get married, and then we're going to southern Africa to launch a ministry school!" His fiancé replied, "I have a business here in the USA, and I know I'm called to do this business. We can visit southern Africa, but I won't live there; I'm not called to do that." He was perplexed. This was not playing out as he imagined. After praying about it, he chose marriage over a ministry school and joined his wife, working in her company.

About ten years later, he had the opportunity to complete a master's in business administration (MBA). While doing this course, he started to build relationships with fellow students who were highly ambitious young professionals from cities across the USA. At the end of a day's class, he would go with them to a bar surrounded by smoke and alcohol, and one by one, they would approach him and have conversations about marriage, money, and success. He got to share godly wisdom, pray for them, and model what a life with Christ looked like. He felt alive! That's when he realized, "I am a missionary! It's nothing like what I imagined, but I'm living out who I was born to be, and it's way more effective than what I originally imagined."

What about you? Where do you have a filter or limited definition of what God is saying to you? What cultural or background experiences cause you to think one thing when God may be saying something completely different? How can you be aware of your filters and ensure that when you hear God, you are hearing clearly? God is so good in leading us despite our ignorance and naivety. However, we can avoid some of the pain or pitfalls if we are diligent in being aware of the filters through which we are hearing.

Shortly after we heard God say to move from California to Pennsylvania, Janine was given a prophetic word by someone who had no idea of what was happening. The prophetic word was, "I see you going on a journey with your family. It's like when you moved from New Zealand to California, but it will be easy this time." Janine was very excited. Here was one of the prophetic confirmations of what we were hearing and a reassurance that it would be easy. Most of all, we were delighted that "it would be easy." We had a picture in our minds of what that meant. Our filter translated this to mean we would sell our dream house quickly and at a high price. We would find a similar home in Pennsylvania quickly, and the move would be smooth. Surely, it meant all the details would come together quickly, easily, and affordably. And in our minds, God's Word was that this would be easy!

You may be surprised that this happened outside our expectations. We sold our house in California, but it took longer, required some extra renovations, and returned less than we expected. We moved to Pennsylvania and stayed in three different and expensive vacation rentals as we searched in vain for a new house. We searched for months for our new home and couldn't find one we could afford that felt like home. On top of this, and most painfully, our moving company did a terrible job, resulting in some of our precious belongings being broken, damaged by water and mold, or lost. This was NOT easy!

So, what happened? Did God lie to us? Did the person who gave us the prophetic word get it wrong? Here's what Janine says. "When I got the prophetic word telling me it would be easy, I jumped to some conclusions of what that would look like. My mistake was that I didn't talk to God and ask Him what He meant when He said it would be easy. I jumped into my definition until it just wasn't working anymore. And then I asked Him. When I asked, I sensed He said that it would be easy if I would trust Him that it would all work out. It was an invitation to worry less and trust more. And once I realized what He meant when He said it would be easy, it was. Whenever I felt stressed, and it seemed hard, I remembered it was easy if I trusted. It was a great lesson to remember that a prophetic word is an invitation to further dialogue with the Lord."

Despite the painful experience, we had many wonderful times as a family and received a surprise financial gift from a friend who covered the physical losses. We are now in a beautiful home, and our trust in God and experience of joy in all circumstances has grown exponentially. Compared to moving from New Zealand to California, it was 'easy!'

So, when you hear from God, it is an invitation to continue talking with Him to understand what He is saying. Just like best practice in receiving communication from an important person in your life, take the time to clarify that what you are hearing is what they are saying! Is the image in your mind the image they are painting? God is incredibly good at speaking 'our language,' but sometimes we misinterpret what He is saying in our haste to act. Test what He is saying—dialogue with Him about it. Move forward and continue conversing with Him, checking your assumptions. "Am I experiencing what you were saying?"

God is good, and He works all things for good. He will get you where you are meant to be going, but we can surely avoid some painful pitfalls and delays if we remove our filters along the way.

ACTIVATION:

Hearing God Through Our Filters

We grew up in New Zealand with English as our first language. But in the USA, despite English being the first language, some exact words have different meanings! We need to be aware of this as we converse with people.

What about you? Reflect and write down some things that may influence how you see and hear. Where did you grow up? What were the accepted cultural norms and sayings? What unique things about how you grew up influence or filter the way you think? What are some of the words you already know have multiple or mixed meanings?

Pause and ask God to talk to you about other things that may have filtered how you see and hear. Coming from New Zealand means we sometimes think smaller than we need to. Coming from a place of poverty (thinking or financially) means we sometimes think from a lack rather than abundance.

What has God been saying to you that may have a different meaning than you have assumed? Take time to ask Him to bring to your memory or attention anything you need to hear or understand differently. Now, ask Him to clarify what He was saying to you. Consider doing this with a wise counselor who can give you a different perspective.

Knowing what you know now, how could you approach your situation differently?

CHAPTER NINE:

Am I Just Hearing What I Want to Hear?

How do you know you genuinely hear God, or are you simply hearing what you want to hear? A few years ago, a friend asked Andy to borrow some money. We had significant cash on hand because of a recent house sale and were renting for a year before making another purchase. Andy's friend said they only needed to borrow some cash for a month. The borrowing was required to cover a cashflow shortfall before receiving funds from a business startup that would easily repay the debt. Andy knew other people involved in the business startup and had no hesitation concerning their character and integrity. We were aligned in vision and values, and the business startup would greatly benefit the community we served.

Andy told Janine, "They asked for $20,000 as a bridging loan for just one month." Janine responded, "Are you sure? What does God say?" Andy answered, "Yeah, I'm sure. This is my friend, and we're on the same page." He gave more of the supporting details. Finally, Janine agreed, saying, "I'm not happy with $20,000, but let's do $10,000." She was reluctant, but because Andy had said he was sure it was God, she agreed to go along with it.

One month later, the friend returned saying, "I'm sorry, I don't have the money. Things didn't quite go as planned, but it will all happen soon." Three months later, we discovered our friends had defaulted on their house payments before even asking us to cover the 'one-month' cash shortfall. If we had done more due diligence at the start, we would have known that lending them money was not wise. In fact, by lending the cash, we had further enabled their financial dysfunction.

Did Andy ask God or follow his own 'good' desire, assuming God agreed? Did Andy truly hear God say to lend them the money? In hindsight, Andy would say, "No." So, what happened to bring Andy to a place where he believed he had heard God? How did he sense he was hearing God but was wrong? What can we learn so that we don't do this again?!

In this instance, Andy was listening to his soul more than the voice of God. He desperately wanted to help his friend and felt compassion for their family. Andy had the means and the motive and needed agreement from Janine. He couldn't imagine saying 'no' to a good friend with whom Andy had invested time and shared vision. Unconsciously, Andy was taking the place of God by being the rescuer and deliverer rather than pausing to seek God's heart in the matter sincerely. In hastily providing the solution himself, avoiding the discomfort of delay or disagreement with a friend, Andy revealed the idol of his heart – "My will, my comfort, my way, be done today." Ouch!

> *"Therefore speak to them, and say to them, 'Thus says the Lord God: Everyone of the house of Israel who sets up idols in his heart, and puts before him what causes him to stumble into iniquity, and then comes to the prophet, I the Lord will answer him who comes, according to the multitude of his idols."*
> *(Ezekiel 14:4)*

God says that if we approach Him with a question but have an idol in our hearts—something we prefer or desire above God—He will answer us according to our idol. This is scary! We will hear God answer us, but the answer will not be the will of God. And the consequence of not following the will of God always ends in a mess. So, how do we know if we have an idol in our hearts? And what do we do about it?

Before we unpack the 'prevention,' know we all make mistakes. It's part of our imperfect nature and why we all need a Savior. The good news is good news! God is gracious and kind and slow to anger (see Exodus 34:6-7). When we confess our sins, He is faithful and just to forgive us and cleanse us of our unrighteousness (see 1 John 1:9). This means acknowledging our mistake, confessing this to God and those our behavior has affected, asking for forgiveness and receiving the grace to start again with a clean slate. It also means changing our thinking to avoid repeating the same thing. Now, how do we change our thinking and approach so that we have a tender heart for hearing God and don't find ourselves hearing what we want to hear?

Psalm 139 gives us an answer.

> *"Search me, O God, and know my heart; try me, and know my anxieties; and see if there is any wicked way in me, and lead me in the way everlasting."*
> *(Psalm 139:23-24)*

The Psalmist invites God to search him, know him, and lead him, now and always, in the eternally true way. In other words, "Hey God, I don't want to be led astray by any idols in my heart. Search me, and if you find any idols, let me know so I can take them down and put you back in the preeminent place in my life." If we stay humble and connected to God and follow the path of wisdom, we will be protected from the deception of only hearing what we want to hear and ending up in a mess.

The money we loaned to our friends was eventually paid back over 18 months. It was a painful lesson for Andy to realize that he only heard what he wanted to hear. It was also a painful confrontation with our friends who had lied to us, knowing from the start that they could not have repaid the borrowing in a month. Andy's part was to search his heart and ask God to reveal what led to this.

Here are some practical ways to keep you from only hearing what you want to hear:

1. Make humility a core value.

Stay humble and easily adjustable. Even if you believe you are hearing God, how open are you to testing and examining that? We have all experienced people who are not humble. They convince themselves they have heard God correctly, refuse to listen to any feedback, and everyone around them can see that they are about to do something stupid. "God told me, so I'm going to do it no matter what anyone says."

Leading a conversation with, "God told me..." is not helpful if you want to receive candid feedback. If you start with "God told me...." anyone who disagrees with you disagrees with God. Instead, use a phrase like, "This is what I believe (or think) I am hearing God say. What do you think? What questions do you have? What feedback would you give me?" You are much more likely to get some candid feedback in the areas of your blind spots when you exhibit humility. Then, respond humbly after receiving feedback with something like, "Thank you for your input. I will talk to God about this and search my heart."

"God resists the proud but gives grace to the humble." (James 4:6)

2. Test your conviction.

Do you believe this is right, or are you simply feeling compassion for the situation?

Conviction is a positive motivation that drives action based on belief. It sounds like, "This is simply the right thing to do, regardless of how it looks or feels." Compassion is sympathy that results in action. Neither of these is wrong, but if you are uncertain whether you are hearing God, check your motivation. How deep is your conviction that this is the right thing to do? What is your conviction regarding this being the will of God? How much are you responding out of compassion for the situation or person?

If you test what you are thinking and find that it is something other than conviction, acknowledge it. "I am being moved by compassion." This is okay and is a valuable understanding and context from which to decide.

3. Give it time and know your decision-making history.

When you feel the urgency or pressure to decide or act, pause. Most times, when we feel pressured to act quickly, we are motivated by fear—fear of missing out, displeasing someone we love or respect, or disconnection.

Especially with more significant decisions, we encourage you to wait for 24 hours. Write the question down and sleep on it. Give yourself time to thoroughly think it over and notice what happens while you wait. After sleeping on it, do you continue to have that same level of conviction? Does the urgency disappear, and you even forget about the situation by the next day? If so, this is good feedback!

Additionally, knowing your decision-making history is essential. What can you learn from your history of decision-making? What happened the last time you felt great urgency or pressure to decide or act quickly? Did it turn out to be God or just an idea that seemed reasonable then? What were the historical indicators that confirmed a decision was following God's voice? Can you recognize those indicators now?

4. Cultivate a close circle of truth-tellers.

"Faithful are the wounds of a friend, but the kisses of an enemy are deceitful." (Proverbs 27:6)

Who around you can speak the truth, even if it is difficult or painful? Who do you have around you that can disagree with you? In the story above, Janine was hesitant. She is usually a truth-teller, but she didn't speak up because Andy said he felt it was God. Janine couldn't understand why she was hesitant, and Andy was very convincing with supporting information that seemed to make sense. Andy needed to pause and give more room for his trusted truth-teller to speak up, especially when she hesitated. Usually, we have agreed to wait until we both have a sense of release or peace. In this case, we didn't follow the peace, and Andy disabled his truth-teller because he didn't want to hear what she had to say.

5. Do your due diligence.

When Jesus was sending out the twelve apostles ahead of Him into Israelite cities, He gave them explicit instructions, including:

"Behold, I send you out as sheep in the midst of wolves. Therefore be wise as serpents and harmless as doves." (Matthew 10:16)

It's no different with us today. Wherever you go and whatever you do, be aware that people tend to be wolf-like – appearing one way but with hidden motives to eat you!

Unfortunately, many of us have fully embraced being innocent and harmless but have ignored the first statement, leaving us naïve and gullible. Jesus commanded, "...be wise as serpents." This means to be shrewd, wary, and prudent. Use your discernment. Sleep with your eyes open! Do your due diligence! Kindly ask the hard questions. Don't be moved by the impulse of the moment. Pause, reflect, and check your assumptions. Is this God? If it truly is, it will easily withstand any question or examination. Wise stewards of Kingdom resources are careful, knowing the value of what they carry.

6. Protect the right agreement(s).

Whatever decision you make, it will affect people. Who do you have a relationship with that this potential decision will affect? They are the stakeholders in the decision that you're making. So, are they aware, and are you in agreement with them?

If you hear one thing and your spouse or covenant partner hears something different, pause. Wait until you agree because once there is unity, God commands a blessing (see Psalm 133). God doesn't bless disunity. Wait and patiently work through the details until you agree before moving forward. If you get to an impasse, seek wise counsel.

ACTIVATION:

Am I Just Hearing What I Want to Hear?

We don't always hear perfectly. We trust that we're hearing God and walking the best we know how, but we know that we hear and see in part. That is why we need the body of believers all around us.

The painful and beautiful thing about our Christian history is the amount of messed up people who cry out to God in the pain of their consequences, and God hears, heals, and restores. The moment we start to think we are fail-proof is when we are lining up for failure! We will make mistakes. And we serve an out-of-this-world God who is merciful and gracious, longsuffering and abounding in goodness and truth, keeping mercy for thousands, forgiving iniquity and transgression and sin... (see Exodus 34:6,7). Our smartest response is to be quick to respond, lean into Him, and continually grow in His ways.

Step 1: Heart check

In reading this chapter, have you become aware of a situation where you have listened to your voice rather than the voice of God? Pause right now and walk through the simple steps of acknowledging where you were wrong, confessing this to God, and, where appropriate to those you did wrong to, asking for forgiveness and forgiving yourself!

Ask the Holy Spirit if there is anything you need to do to put it right. We encourage you to share this with an independent, wise counselor to navigate the proper process and timing of restoration (and confrontation where necessary).

Step 2: Setting yourself up to succeed in hearing well:

Let's review the six steps outlined in this chapter and score ourselves from 1 to 10, with 10 being the goal for healthy and confident hearing God in big decisions.

- *Embracing Humility*
  "I could be wrong; I am open to adjustment."

- *Motivated by Conviction*
  "This is God – it's the right thing to do."

- *Prepared to Pause*
  "I'm going to give this 24hrs."

- *Unfiltered Feedback From Truth-Teller(s)*
  "I got candid input from a third party."

- *Doing Full Due Diligence*
  "I asked and checked all the facts."

- *In Proper Agreement(s)*
  "I am in full agreement with the stakeholders."

Which of these are you doing well? What area is the most significant area for growth? What's one thing you can do today to start implementing growth?

Step 3: Strengthening your circle of wise counselors and truth-tellers

We want to re-emphasize this point because it is the most common weakness and, by far, the best path toward robust decision-making in hearing God.

- Who could you start to build a regular connection with, where you commit to one another to speak 100% truth?

- If you can't think of someone, don't worry; it only takes one person to initiate. Pray now and ask the Holy Spirit, "Who could I begin to build that kind of relationship with? Who could I invite?"

- If you have someone, when did you last ask them for candid feedback on what you were hearing and your decisions? Call them and tell them about this book and that you are looking to strengthen the connection. Appreciate them and commit to guarding one another's back. Agree to regularly touch base and ask one another the questions most people lack the courage to ask!

CHAPTER TEN:

Staying Aware of the Big Picture

As we seek to hear God for the specific details of our task, we must also stay aware of the big picture. The general focus of a results-oriented marketplace professional is... results. We want to know what to do, and we tend towards action. As we listen for God's direction, we are constantly looking toward the practical action steps we can take in alignment with this. While in that process, we can get so focused on the details that we get lost in the 'now' and lose sight of the big picture. We also need to learn to pause during all that we are doing and remember that God is weaving together a masterpiece!

> *"For we are His workmanship, created in Christ Jesus for good works, which God prepared beforehand that we should walk in them." (Ephesians 2:10)*

Imagine you are walking through a forest. You step over roots, stoop under branches, and move around each tree on your way to a distant location. That's like learning to hear God's voice daily, especially during a challenge.

Now, imagine you are lifted in a helicopter over the forest. The elevation enables you to see the entire panorama. Your perspective changes as you see the end goal, releasing encouragement, clarity, and momentum.

During a challenging time, when Andy was surrounded by a forest of opportunity and uncertainty, he felt overwhelmed. Many people gave him different advice, suggesting endless books to read and directions to take. Andy was putting together new content and designing new courses and was overly busy. Andy's daily practice is journalling – writing down thoughts and insights from hearing God's voice while reading Scripture.

One day, Andy decided to read back over the previous month of journaling and see what he had been hearing. As he reflected, it became apparent there was an overall picture he had been missing. He had been focused on all the different pieces - the detailed steps - and while each was good on its own, it was a whole other picture together. As Andy reflected overall, he saw the goodness of God weaving all the details together. Andy could now see how God had placed all the people and resources around him to produce a masterful picture!

So, how do you see the big picture while staying focused on the detailed task at hand?

1. Pause.

"Be still, and know that I am God..." (Psalm 46:10)

Andy loves to trail run. The trail at the back of our house was steep and rocky. If he didn't pay absolute attention to the trail, he would constantly stumble and hurt himself. One day, Andy sensed God was inviting Him to walk instead of run. Initially, he didn't appreciate the slower pace, but gradually, he became aware of a perspective that was impossible to see while traveling fast. No longer focused on his feet, Andy noticed the different trees and landscape and heard a range of birds that had been there all along! Slowing down revealed a beauty he had been missing.

For all of us, the first step in staying aware of the big picture is to slow down. Pause. Stop. Intentionally lift your eyes to see what is all around you. On the journey of hearing God at work, this is where daily journaling, processing, and recording what you are hearing is invaluable.

Here are some practical steps to help you pause, slow down, and position yourself for a different perspective:

- Go for a walk or run or bike.

- Sit in a garden or a place with a garden view.

- Intentionally focus on what you can see, smell, and hear.

- Take deep breaths, counting to three as you inhale, hold, and exhale.

- Do a physical workout to get some of the pent-up energy out of your system.

- Pause and become aware of what you sense in your thoughts and spirit.

2. Reflect.

Take time to reflect on the lessons you have been learning and what God has been doing on your behalf. Go back over your journal and write down a summary of what you have been hearing over the last 30 days. Use the following questions to stimulate a conversation with God:

What Have I Been Learning?
About God? About Myself?

What could God have been teaching me this season that I could never have learned if the situation or circumstances were different?

What Is Really Going On?

Be aware that much more is going on than what involves you. Pain or adversity tends to get us focused on ourselves. If you step back and look around, is something much bigger at play? Rather than looking at what is not happening, reframe the question to say, "What is happening?"

Are the Seemingly Different Situations Interconnected?

Are the situations you walk through personally and professionally different aspects of the same lesson? Is there a repeated lesson, opportunity, or conflict?

What Have I Been Hearing?

Review the last few weeks or months and summarize your hearing. Have there been repeated words or themes?

Who Has God Sent to Help Me on the Journey?

Consider the people around you – not those demanding your time and attention, but those one step outside your immediate circle who have offered help or advice. How have you responded? Are you avoiding or prioritizing wise counselors?

What Has God Done on My Behalf?

As you reflect and remember, what do you see that God has rescued and redeemed you from? What things has He taken care of? Where has He worked things for good? How can you turn that into gratitude?

As you reflect on the situation overall, what themes emerge? What is the bigger picture being revealed?

3. Refocus.

Now that you have taken a moment to be still and reflect on the possible bigger picture, how has your perspective changed? What is clearer? What do you need to stop doing, start doing, and keep doing? How will you stay focused on the day-to-day while keeping the big picture in mind? When will you next take an intentional pause?

CHAPTER ELEVEN:

What to Do When You Hear Nothing

At the start of this book, we established that we hear more of God than we realize. Most of us need to slow down more and listen! As we build on this truth and you work through the activation exercises in each chapter, you will experience a greater connection with God and clarity in hearing His voice. But what do you do if you follow all you know to do, yet you don't seem to hear anything? What if we only hear silence?

Here are some keys we have learned that will encourage and help when you don't sense you are hearing anything:

1. Keep walking and growing in godly character.

"Yes, Lord, walking in the way of your laws, we wait for you; your name and renown are the desire of our hearts." (Isaiah 26:8 NIV)

We 'wait' *as* we walk. This means continuing to do what we know to do while also continuing to listen for God's voice, however, and whenever He wants to speak.

God is maturing His sons and daughters who hear His voice and know His heart – they represent His character well. He is not seeking to train servants or slaves who must be constantly told how to think and what to do.

When you are a mature child of God, you don't have to ask Him for instructions or directions at every step. If you know His heart and walk in His character, keep walking! So, if you are walking in His ways and seeking to honor Him in all you do and don't hear anything, trust that you are walking the right way.

"For all creation is waiting eagerly for that future day when God will reveal who his children really are." (Romans 8:19 NLT)

2. Make the decision, and keep listening.

We grow in relationship as we grow in trust; trust in God and ourselves. Kris Vallotton says, "You were saved when you believed in Jesus, but you were transformed when you realized He believed in you." In the process of growing in trust, we must make decisions. If God decided everything for us, we would remain immature and incapable of governing anything. He desires that we grow to rule and reign with Him, which requires that we grow in decision-making!

When Andy was asking God if he was to marry Janine, to his frustration, he did not hear a clear "yes" or "no." He only heard silence regarding that question! However, God did speak a Scripture:

"Your ears shall hear a word behind you, saying, 'This is the way, walk in it,' whenever you turn to the right hand or whenever you turn to the left." (Isaiah 30:21)

What was immediately apparent was that the voice (word) was from behind him, redirecting as necessary. Andy wanted a voice out in front, clearly deciding because Andy didn't want to get it wrong. God wanted Andy to grow in maturity and trust and make the decision. Twenty-five years later, Andy can resoundingly say he made a great choice!

As we grow in God's ways, we develop confidence in making decisions, even in silence. As we follow through on our decision, continuing to listen for God's voice, He will redirect or realign us as necessary. Trust God. Trust also that God trusts you.

3. Remember the last thing you heard.

Sometimes, when we don't hear anything, it's because we have yet to follow through on the last thing we heard. Have you ever given someone advice, and shortly after that, they return for more advice but haven't done anything with what you already said? Do you want to give them more advice, or will you wait until they do something with what you have already said? What will help them grow the most?

It is often the same with us and God. He has already told us what to do, so when we return and ask again, He says nothing. Go back to what you last heard God say. Have you obeyed? Have you obeyed fully?

4. Review what He has been saying: Find the theme.

As mentioned in an earlier chapter, there may be a recurring theme in what God is talking to you about. When we value what He has said, it often leads to fresh revelation through those words.

One time, when Andy thought God wasn't speaking, he noticed hummingbirds everywhere. They appeared throughout a new book, constantly showing up outside whatever window he was at, and even got a mention in different conversations. One such conversation referred to hummingbirds as a symbol of a messenger from God. Initially, Andy was excited, but then he realized he already knew what God would say. Why? Because God had been saying the same thing in many ways all along. Andy just needed to act on it. He had the confidence to act on it once he recognized the theme of what God was doing and saying. Value what God has already said, and you will receive more.

5. Seek a different perspective.

When we are in a difficult time or a place where we are making a big decision, especially with big stakes, it is sometimes hard to be confident we are hearing God. There is emotion involved and maybe past bad experiences. It's great in those moments to talk to a wise counselor. Go to them and ask for candid feedback. Make sure that it is somebody who fits the description of a wise counselor from chapter two. Tell them the situation and get them to give you some candid feedback. Invite them to tell you the hard things. What does their perspective add to your situation? Is there a different way of looking at things you have not yet seen? Does God want to speak to you through this perspective?

6. Celebrate the journey and the progress you've made.

Life is a journey, and you have made progress. God has been with you thus far and will never leave you alone. He is in your future, waiting for you as much as He is with you right now. You can trust Him to get you to that future. Reflect on how far you have come, and He has been with you. Sometimes, when we feel like we can't hear Him, we get anxious. It's good to remember that He has spoken and led us in the past and will do it again.

ACTIVATION:

What to Do When You Hear Nothing

Reflection questions:

- Ask the Lord if He trusts you. Meditate on the answer and reflect on what that means to you.

- Is there a step you already know to take? What is holding you back from taking that step? Talk with the Lord about what is holding you back. Get help if you need to.

- Go back to the last thing you know you heard from the Lord. Have you responded to that word? What do you need to do?

- Check for a theme in what the Lord is saying. Is there something that you have been missing?

- Find a wise counselor and ask for candid feedback on your situation. What does their perspective add?

- Celebrate your progress and the fact that He is with you. Meditate on the fact that He is faithful to lead and guide you into a great future.

CHAPTER TWELVE:

Hearing God With Others

We are not called to do much of what we do alone. God has set us in a community so that we will impact one another's lives. Whether it's your boss, your spouse, your children, or others in your community, we are called to do this together. This sounds wonderful, but how does this work when you think you hear something from God and your business partners, spouse, or children don't hear the same thing? Here are five prerequisites or heart attitudes to check and align so that your hearing God with others is a mutually beneficial and fruitful experience!

1. Embrace humility.

> *"But He gives more grace. Therefore He says: 'God resists the proud, but gives grace to the humble.' Therefore submit to God. Resist the devil and he will flee from you." (James 4:6-7)*

No matter who you are working with, if you don't walk humbly, you are in danger of having God resist you! It is far better to walk humbly, knowing that God will give you grace to navigate the situation. What does that look like? Humility means you are not elevating your status above the status of others. As C.S. Lewis said, "Humility is not thinking less of yourself; it's thinking of yourself less." It means approaching a conversation confidently and knowing, "I might be wrong. There may be a better way."

2. Walk in love.

> *"Though I speak with the tongues of men and of angels, but have not love, I have become sounding brass or a clanging cymbal."* (1 Corinthians 13:1)

Even if you are 'right' and accurately hear the Lord say something, if your actions aren't done from a heart of love, you are like someone speaking while banging pots and pans together. In other words, nobody wants to hear or even be near you! In all His interactions, Jesus kept love at the center. He was always right, yet He never lorded it over people or made anyone feel small around Him. He always treated people with love and dignity. It's much easier to hear hard things from someone you know loves you than from someone who doesn't. Sometimes, when we try to get our point across, people can't hear us because we sound like a clanging cymbal.

3. Be patient.

> *"Love suffers long and is kind; love does not envy; love does not parade itself, is not puffed up…"* (1 Corinthians 13:4)

Give people the time and space to hear God for themselves. Often, we get excited when God speaks a new idea or direction to us. We rush out and tell the other invested parties but may get a poor or less-than-excited response. We think, "I know that I heard from God; why won't they get on board?" Sometimes, we are moving ahead of God and haven't given the people around us time to ask or hear God for themselves.

When we heard from God that we were moving from California to the east coast of the USA, our 21-year-old came home from church to listen to us discussing a new location to live. When she had left for church that morning, there was no thought of any possibility that we would be moving. She was shocked at our sudden exploration of a significant change. She wasn't resistant to God; she needed time to hear from God herself. Give people time to listen for themselves and be aware they might hear differently from you.

4. Being 'right' isn't the goal.

Jesus is always our example of perfect theology and perfect Kingdom living. In walking out agreement and unity with others, Jesus chose to be mistreated, misunderstood, and betrayed rather than initiating a broken relationship. Jesus decided to be wronged rather than saying, "No, I'm right; you are all wrong." For the sake of connection with us, He chose to go to the cross despite knowing He was perfect, He was right, and He had the power to do something different. For the sake of love, He chose to go to the cross. So, how about you? What is most important? Is it being right and proving yourself, or is it the relationship? Don't lose the relationship over something that has only temporal value. Pause, wait. Ask yourself, "Will this matter in a day, month, or year?"

5. It's okay to disagree.

Disagreement is not the same as dishonor or disrespect. I can respectfully disagree with you while protecting your dignity. Disagreement means I don't agree with you on a particular matter. With most things, we can still walk together and work together even if we see certain things differently.

How easily can people around you disagree with you? This is called confrontation; when done well, it is a necessary part of healthy teams and relationships. If we only have people around us who agree with us, we will become siloed, small, and in danger of walking into error!

It's one thing to have a culture where people can respectfully disagree with you; it's another to develop the courage and confidence required to disagree respectfully with someone in authority. Andy grew up with a strong preference for conflict avoidance. To grow as a leader, he had to grow in healthy confrontation. This has required a change in belief and the development of some better communication skills.

Andy's belief around disagreement and confrontation changed when he had a revelation that even God allowed us to disagree with Him respectfully! In Exodus 32, Moses humbly disagreed with God. The Israelites had just made a gold calf, making a sacrifice to it and saying it had rescued them from Egypt. God saw this and said to Moses, "These people of yours are stiff-necked and stubborn; leave Me alone, I will destroy them and make of you (Moses) a great nation." Moses immediately pleaded with God, saying, "Wait a moment, God. It's not a good idea to destroy them. These are your people that you rescued from Egypt. If you destroy your people, the Egyptians will say that you rescued them only to kill them in the wilderness. Turn from your anger and change your mind concerning this evil against your people." (See Exodus 32:1-14)

That is called a disagreement! Moses respectfully confronted God. And God changed His mind concerning what He would do to the Israelites. Wow, that is influence! If Moses could respectfully disagree with the most powerful being in the entire universe, how much more so could we respectfully disagree with one another, regardless of position?

The second aspect of healthy confrontation is HOW to disagree. It can be difficult in the moment, and some of us must gather our thoughts clearly before conversing. So here are some phrases that can help buy you some time and lead to sharing your difference of opinion:

- "I'm not sure I agree with you; let me think about it."
- "Is it possible that you're not hearing this right?"
- "May I give you a different opinion?"
- "Is it possible that there's a different way of looking at it?"

Crucial Conversations: Tools for Talking When Stakes are High, by Grenny, Patterson, and others, is a good resource for developing this area.

When hearing God with others, we must walk humbly lest God oppose us. It is essential to walk in love; otherwise, we are just noisy gongs or pots and pans. We must also be open to being confronted and having people disagree.

What to Do if You Disagree but Need to Decide?

Sometimes, disagreement persists, and a time-bound decision must be made. This could be purchasing a property, hiring someone for a specific role, or taking on a new opportunity. No action could result in a missed opportunity. Action may result in an undue burden for one of the parties. You may be able to live with a missed opportunity. But what if that opportunity is (or feels like) life and death for one of the parties involved? Assuming you have already checked off the heart attitudes listed above, seeking an independent, wise counselor is essential.

Despite our best intentions, this has happened in the past and will continue to occur in the future. Consequently, we highly recommend intentionally building a relationship with an independent and trusted wise counselor before any disagreement. Then, when you need them in a critical, highly emotional moment in the future, the relationship and decision-making process are already established.

When working in banking as a business manager, Andy used to call this an 'Exit Agreement.' It was a pre-established course of mediation, action, or decision-making process should two or more business partners get to an impasse. This is especially important when those two parties are friends, doing business together, and say, 'Oh, that will never happen to us!" If you pay attention now and write out a decision-making process for the 'unlikely' event that does happen, then you are much more likely to protect the relationship and have an outcome that works best for all.

ACTIVATION:
_____

Hearing God With Others

If we want to live a life of meaning and influence beyond ourselves, we must work with others. Working with others means we will be with people who see, hear, and act differently from us. Assuming we all start on the same page and think we are heading in the same direction, if there is more than one of us, there will be more than one pathway forward. So, how do we do that well?

Step 1: Reflect on the five heart attitudes and approach to hearing God with others:

- Humility – "I may be wrong."

- Love – "My behavior and interaction communicate value for others."

- Patience – "I'm willing to wait and give you time to process this."

- Being right vs. protecting relationship – "Will this decision still be more important than your connection with the other person a day, a week, or a year from now?"

- Respectful disagreement – "How easily and safely can people disagree with me?"

Where must you grow in belief, attitude, and behavior regarding hearing God with others?

Where do you need to grow in speaking up and contributing your voice to the conversation? What will you do about that, and when?

Step 2: Whose Voice Have You Turned Down?

Pause for a moment. Consider the people and situations around you. How easily is it for people to disagree with you?

What happened to the last person who spoke up with a different opinion? How long ago was that?

Is there anyone whose voice you are turning down?

Ask God to show you how you are listening and responding to the voices of people He has placed around you. If you realize you have reduced the volume of those voices or removed yourselves from those connections, repent before God. Then, go to that person(s) and acknowledge what you did, asking them how your behavior affected them, asking for forgiveness, and making a plan to protect the volume of their voice in the future.

> *"I do not pray for these alone, but also for those who will believe in Me through their word; that they all may be one, as You, Father, are in Me, and I in You; that they also may be one in Us, that the world may believe that you sent Me." (John 17:21)*

Summary and Next Steps

Congratulations on completing this book. We are grateful you are willing to invest in yourself and the people around you by leaning in to *listen up* and hear more of God in all of life! Please know that we have been praying for you. We trust that your walk with God has grown significantly through these pages as your confidence in knowing Him and His Voice has increased. So, where to from here? Here are a few things we want you to remember:

Embrace the journey.

This is not about perfection; it is about growth. You won't always get it right, but you will grow in knowing God is speaking and being easily moved by Him in every area of your life. Embrace the journey, fully immerse yourself daily in His Word, and intentionally surround yourself with wise counsel. And keep walking!

Be quick to respond.

Whether you hear affection, correction, or direction, respond quickly. It is not your ability to hear; it's what you do with what you hear that matters. Your response to what you hear and your (quick) timing are essential. Faith (or hearing God) without action is phony (see James 3:14-26). So, be quick to respond.

Build a lifestyle, not a transaction.

Hearing God is a relationship, not a transaction or an event. Prioritize time daily for 1:1 time with Him and His Word. And keep the communication lines open 24/7. Cultivate an awareness or sensitivity that God is speaking more than we realize because His heart and desire are for you. The most incredible privilege of humanity is a personal relationship with our Father in Heaven. Build a lifelong relationship of ever-increasing connection with Him, not a transactional task list to complete.

Manage the noise.

The explosion of technology and our instant access to the world of connections and information are both benefits and vulnerabilities. There is more atmospheric noise today than when Jesus walked the earth! If you don't manage the noise, it will manage you. Be intentional about choosing what, who, when, and how much you listen. Be aware of all the noises competing for your attention. And make your greatest priority being still to know God (see Psalm 46:10).

Multiply what you have learned.

One of the best ways to reinforce and retain learning is by sharing what we learn. Consider using this book with a friend or a small cohort to gather and discuss the activation exercises together. Join us through HopeDirective.com to translate and distribute resources like this to those with limited access. Follow our story and share your own on social media @HeaveninBusiness.

May you grow from strength to strength in your walk with God. May you experience the awe and joy of following His Voice. May you find and fulfill all that you were born for. May your life demonstrate to the world around you what is possible for ordinary people who have a relationship with an extraordinary God. May history record you as a friend of God.

We can't wait to hear your stories!

Andy and Janine Mason

Recommended Resources

These are all by authors we trust and will help you grow in your relationship through hearing God's voice.

- *Take Another Look at Guidance: Discerning the Will of God*
  by Bob Mumford (1993)

- *Four Keys to Hearing God's Voice*
  by Mark and Patti Virkler (2013)

- *The Good Fight: Prophetic Processing Workbook*
  by Dan McCollam (2017)

- *How to Hear God at Work*
  by Matthew Flegler (2021)

- *Hearing God: Developing a Conversational Relationship With God*
  by Dallas Willard (2021)

- *Created to Hear God*
  by Havilah Cunnington (2023)

- *Vox Dei Prophetic eCourse*
  by Julian C. Adams. JulianAdams.org/VoxDei

OTHER BOOKS:

By Andy and Janine Mason

- *Dream Culture: Bringing Dreams to Life (2011)*

- *God With You at Work (2014)*

- *Kingdom Tools for Teaching: Heavenly Strategies for Real Classrooms (2015)*

- *Finding Hope in Crazy Times: Daily Stories of Hearing God (2019)*

About the Authors

Andy and Janine Mason are dynamic and passionate authors, speakers, and mentors dedicated to helping individuals and organizations realize their full potential. With a deep-seated belief in the transformative power of a personal walk with God in all of life, they have co-authored several impactful books, including *"Dream Culture: Bringing Dreams to Life," "God with You at Work," "Finding Hope in Crazy Times,"* and *"Kingdom Tools for Teachers."*

Andy and Janine are the founders of HeaveninBusiness.com, an initiative that integrates faith and the workplace, providing practical tools and spiritual insights for entrepreneurs and business leaders. Their combined experience spans over two decades, during which they have empowered countless individuals through their workshops, retreats, and personal coaching sessions.

With a background in agriculture, finance, and business consultancy, Andy brings a pragmatic approach to their teachings. His expertise in strategic planning and leadership development has been instrumental in guiding many to success in both personal and professional realms.

With her rich experience in education and mentoring, Janine adds a nurturing and insightful perspective to their work. Her ability to connect with people personally and her deep understanding of spiritual principles make her a trusted speaker, beliefs coach, and mentor.

Andy and Janine Mason are committed to inspiring hope, fostering growth, and equipping people with the tools they need to navigate life's challenges and achieve their dreams. Their work continues to impact lives globally, encouraging a culture where dreams are not just imagined but brought to life.

Tune in to their weekly podcast, Authentic Conversations around the messy intersection of faith, family, and business, on your favorite podcast platform.

For questions, testimonies, and requests, you can email:

contact@HeaveninBusiness.com

Made in the USA
Middletown, DE
10 September 2024

60094699R10099